Wishing
for Wings

Wishing for Wings

by Debbie Jacob

IAN RANDLE PUBLISHERS

Kingston • Miami

First published in Jamaica, 2013 by
Ian Randle Publishers
11 Cunningham Avenue
Box 686
Kingston 6
www.ianrandlepublishers.com

ISBN 978-976-637-802-8

NATIONAL LIBRARY OF JAMAICA CATALOGUING-IN-PUBLICATION DATA

   Jacob, Debbie
     Wishing for wings / Debbie Jacob

     p. ; cm

   Based on the author's experience of teaching CXC English
   to seven young men in the Youth Training Centre

   ISBN 978-976-637-802-8 (pbk)

   1. Juvenile delinquents – Education – Trinidad and Tobago
   2. Teacher-student relationships

   I. Title

   373.72983 dc 23

Publisher's Note: For many reasons outlined near the end of the book, the
author has decided to use only the revised work of her students. Although
students spoke Creole, and at least one student in the final class spoke only
Creole, she has included only the revised work in formal English.

Image pages vi-vii © Julian Kaufman
Cover and Book Design by Ian Randle Publishers

Printed and Bound in the USA

For the young men in my CXC English Language class who gave me the most incredible experience of my life, and for Donna McDonald who believed in all of us.

Contents

Dreams

by Langston Hughes

Hold fast to dreams

For if dreams die

Life is a broken-winged bird

That cannot fly.

Hold fast to dreams

For when dreams go

Life is a barren field

Frozen with snow.

New Beginnings

*Miss Pope from Bishop Anstey High School East had
been calling me religiously for at least a year before I finally
gave in. She wanted me to teach CXC English language
to some teenage boys and young men who desperately
needed an English teacher. None of them were attending
secondary school.*

"You will enjoy working with these young men," she
said. "They are respectful, eager to learn, but they can't
find anyone to help them. Call Donna McDonald. She will
arrange for you to meet them."

Miss Pope happened to contact me on the right day. I
had always argued that I could not afford any free work, but
on that day, there seemed to be something more important
in this world than money.

Something told me a little community service would
be good for the soul. After all, these were young men who
wanted to learn English, a subject that most boys seem to
scorn these days. No one forced them to take an English
class – not even their mothers.

I called Ms McDonald after I spoke to Ms Pope. She
arranged for a meeting the same day I called her, and she
enlisted me in her cause immediately. I had no time to think
about what I was doing, and if the truth were known, I really
didn't want to think about anything.

I missed my daughter, Ijanaya, who had gone away to
university in the US. I needed a project to keep me busy
because I didn't want to think about the possibility of her
not coming back home to Trinidad and Tobago after she
finished school. My bull terrier, Jada, had been killed in a

dog fight in my own yard, so my home no longer felt like a sanctuary. I needed somewhere to go. I needed…something. What that something was I didn't know at the time.

"Do you need to see my résumé?" I asked Ms McDonald.

"No," she said.

"My teacher registration number? My degrees?"

"Not necessary," she said.

"By the way, I have degrees in anthropology and education; a certificate in library science – but I don't have any degree in English," I said. "I taught English for 16 years, but that really came out of my background in journalism."

The more I spoke, the worse I thought I sounded.

"Doesn't matter," said Ms McDonald. "The only thing I ask is that you stay. Don't quit on them. They can't take that. They've been waiting a long time for an English teacher."

On October 16, 2010, I held my first class. I was scared. I had never taught a CXC English language course before, and I didn't relish the notion that I might let these young men down.

Twenty-seven guys showed up for my assessment to determine who qualified for a CXC level class. None were nerds. They were tough boys – at least on the outside. They came from different communities, mostly poor and rough – the places that the police raid regularly even when there is no curfew.

Only one boy stood out from the sea of serious faces: Jahmai, with his mouth full of gold teeth that he flashed when he smiled. The rest just looked nervous, aloof or puzzled. I wondered what they were thinking. They had only one question for me: "Where are you from, Miss?"

"The States," I said, "but I have lived here for 28 years."

They looked like they didn't know what to think about that, and I certainly didn't know what to say to them.

I had no textbooks yet, but I knew how the class must begin so I handed out and read a passage from *A Moveable Feast* by Ernest Hemingway: "…sometimes when I was starting a new story and I could not get going, I would stand and look out over the roofs of Paris and think, 'Do not worry. You have always written before and you will write now. All you have to do is write one true sentence. Write the truest sentence you know.'"

No one smiled; everyone seemed to ponder Hemingway's advice or maybe they were just thinking about how weird I seemed.

And then I gave them their assessment. My students, who had been sitting like perfect statues, now began to slump, fidget and flash worried frowns. You could cut the tension with a knife as I walked around the room glancing at what they wrote. Most of the students could write basic sentences, but as far as grammar goes, they didn't know how to identify nouns, verbs or any other parts of speech. As they settled to write one true sentence, many students pointed to notes they had written on the bottom of their papers.

Some whispered the message as I passed:

"Please, Miss, tell me what you want me to do. I'll do anything you want. Don't leave us. We've waited a long time to find an English teacher."

That first class, I knew, might just have been an English teacher's dream. My students didn't waste a minute of class time. They were sponges soaking up knowledge. There would be hurdles – like the emotional distance between us – but at least they were willing to learn.

We agreed to meet from 4:00 p.m. to 7:00 p.m. every Saturday evening and from 1:00 p.m. to 3:00 p.m. on Sundays because they wanted to sit the CXC English exam in May.

"That will be trying a t'ing," I said, "because it's two years of work we'll have to cram into eight months."

"We'll do it, Miss," they assured.

That made me feel a twinge of sadness because I knew that meant I'd have to weed out the weak students who could not keep up with the pace.

Who would I choose for this class? All of these teenagers and young men were united in their zeal to learn. They were determined to fight against the odds and the stereotypes that defined them and get passes in English.

Nothing had come easily to these boys in their lives. I knew – indeed I still know – that they are about as far removed from my world, and probably yours, as they could possibly be. What I didn't know at that time, is that they would teach me more than I could ever teach them.

All I could teach them was grammar and how to write an essay. All I could prepare them for was an exam – an exam that in my mind meant little in the scheme of things if you were measuring the real importance of life: a good job, happiness, a purpose in life. But that exam meant everything in the world to them.

They looked to me for help, and why not? Most of the answers I had for life had come out of some book so they must have assumed I had enough book sense to teach them. All of their answers could be found on the street in places that we don't want to acknowledge let alone face because their streets force us to face the unknown.

When I reached home that first night after class, I read their assessments. I couldn't get over the paragraphs they had written about what animals they would choose to be. I thought they would all say lions or tigers – something fierce – but most of them said birds because they could soar above their lives – soar above the problems of Trinidad and Tobago and the world.

If they could look down on the world like a bird, they felt sure they would find it beautiful. Some students wanted to be dogs because they're loyal. And then there was Olton, a weak writer, who had dropped out of school in Form One. He wrote about why he wanted to be a turtle, and that answer blew me away.

I swallowed hard and tried not to cry. I spent the next week gathering the strength to go back to teach again in the Youth Training Centre (YTC) – a euphemism for Trinidad and Tobago's boys' prison.

I Wish...

All the way to YTC, I kept stealing glances at the brown envelope on the seat next to me. That envelope held my students' assessments from the first day of class. Instead of opting for some formal assessment of these students who had volunteered for a CXC English language class, I had made up my own, which I hoped would offer some clues about how much they knew about language – especially grammar, syntax and basic writing structure.

On my way to teach my second class, I felt confused. Ms McDonald had said, "You have to narrow that number of students down to the ones who could do CXC. You can't keep all 27 of those boys. Cut that class at least in half."

"No problem," I promised.

I thought the assessment I gave these boys would help me make a clear decision about which students should remain in the class, but the assessment made the problem worse. Olton impressed me with the most creative answer to the animal question. Yes, Olton mixed up *would* and *will* like most Trinis do because *would* = *will* in Trinidadian creole, but I could fix that.

Only one student, Shawn, wrote enough to demonstrate he could argue a point. The rest seemed to be too guarded for me to truly assess, and I feared they could not score high enough marks on the creative writing unless they could let down their guard.

"You have to make a decision before the third class," Ms McDonald said, "because of the deadline for signing them up for the exam."

I had to get a feel for these distant teenagers – lads as they are called in YTC. Could they write an entire essay? From that paragraph I had given them to write on what animal they wanted to be, there was only one student I knew I wanted for sure: the lad who wanted to be a turtle.

What were they feeling? I had no clue. Which students could make it through the exam? What if I cut someone who could have passed the exam and worse yet, what if I kept lads who couldn't pass because I happen to be a soft touch who is swayed by emotion?

Their stony silence in class gave nothing away about these teenagers. Puzzled about what they took away from Hemingway's advice to write one true sentence, I only knew that exercise seemed to have made them even more guarded or maybe they just didn't realise that assignment was their cue to win me over with the most creative sentences they could write.

I wanted to turn around, go back home, sit on the floor with their papers spread all around me and search a little deeper. Maybe if I read those papers again, I would find something I had missed. Maybe it wouldn't seem that they were hiding more than they were revealing or maybe it wouldn't seem that they were throwing around religion as a shield, something to keep them out of trouble and keep them in everyone's good graces – including mine.

They certainly had learned to play the game of survival in YTC. There, religious jargon is more powerful than bullets, and that, I would have to address. I wanted real feelings and real expression – not religious platitudes.

"What's with all the God talk?" I asked as we settled into that second class.

They all watched me. "I mean, I believe in God. I'm as religious as anyone else, but putting God in every sentence you write or speak is not going to get you a CXC pass."

I could almost hear them breathe. Stony silence once again.

That night, after the second class, I went back to the drawing board. I tossed all the possibilities around in my mind. One by one I tried to match faces with papers. Still, no one besides Shawn and Olton had emerged from the pack so I read every paper yet again, this time facing the fact I'd have to release those whose writing I could barely decipher. Still, I had many possibilities:

1. Jahmai, 18

Presently I now understand my true purpose here at YTC. Before I was lost in the world of wrong-doing but thanks to God and the teachings of my adopted brother I'm on the path to understanding my purpose in this present life.

I would like to be a dog mainly because I believe a dog's life is far from boring. It is also true that he has to face hardship but he is always victorious.

I would not only like to take this class but to pass this class because it is a necessity for me to acquire this subject to progress in my further studies, to acquire my profession of choice.

One true sentence: I enjoy and feel comfortable around my language teacher.

2. Olton

I'm respectful and honest, and I like to have fun.

I will like to be a turtle because I don't want to die at 20 or 30. I want to live to be a thousand years old because I will like to see the different children who will meet on this earth when I'm gone.

The reason why I am taking this class is because I want to be better in life when I go back outside and also I want to hold on to a good job and show everybody I'm a different person.

One true sentence: I am hurt on the inside and happy on the outside and plenty people don't know that but they will know in timing.

3. JR, 18

I like to read. I have a high self-esteem and self control, most importantly I believe that there is a God.

I will love to be a bird, any kind, once I can fly. Just thinking about it makes me want to live like it looking down and sharing the view and breeze.

I have a problem with speaking not only that but analysing questions. In today's society you must be able to explain yourself while conversing and to be understood.

Nicolla, that is her name, and I love her but not more than my mother. That sentence is true because for me it came from my heart.

4. Marc

My real name is Sydney Marc Friday. I am named after my mother. I enjoy writing anything – music, stories, speeches, anything. I spent six years in England from age four to ten and despite my many mistakes I believe in me. I also have to work on my handwriting.

I would like to be a robin. It's a brown bird with red chest. I do not have any special reason for liking this bird but I find that it's rare and unique.

I would like to become a musical artiste because there are many things you could do with words. I simply enjoy reading and writing and learning how to go even deeper is like eating ice cream and cake.

One true sentence: I will feel proud of myself when I complete this exam.

5. Daniel

I have plenty respect for people that is how I grew up. I come from a good home. I love to put my best in what I do. I love to pray and to talk about god and I play rugby and football. I am 18 years old. I left school from Form 4. I would love to be content.

I will like to be a dog a dog have four feet it is short it have eyes, mouth, nose, brain, and it can run fast and it gets on bad for its right and I will like to be that animal because it have understanding and it is a man best friend and it is very good to be around and it thinks just like a man.

I want to take this class because I always like this subject and it can help me in life but I will need help in this class please help me in this class.

One true sentence: I enjoy my class today.

6. Shawn

My name is Shawn. I am 18 years old. In almost all the situations I find myself in I know right from wrong but still choose to do wrong things. I like football and I am good at football. This is not only mines but others people's opinion. I am a lover of money. I don't encourage violence and I am always reluctant to fright or harm someone but know how to hurt somebody and I do hurt people if I see fit. I don't believe it but it best describes me in situations. I get nervous if I have to talk in front of a crowd. I like reading books but only found that out when I got incarcerated. I am also able to get comfortable in almost any situation.

I would like to be an eagle because of its flying ability, which makes it very portable in a short space of time also because an eagle always does the hunting. Eagles are never made preys.

I would like to take this class because I know that I have the ability. Also because at the time I was incarcerated I was in Form 5 in a good school so I was kind of interrupted. Also because I have a plan accomplishing maths is part of that so I have the chance to do part of my plans from in here I will accept the start.

One true sentence: Consequences of contrary actions are inevitable but many times the benefits of those same actions may last forever.

7. Brandon

I am 17 years of age. I love to read and do mathematics. I am a very hard-working person. I am a footballer and a cricketer. I love to cook and bake as well. I am a certified electrician.

If I could be a lion I would be the king of the jungle and any other animal would be scared of me.

I want to take this class to better my speaking and my choice of words to better my reading and writing and my vocabulary.

One true sentence: I talk to a lot of people today.

8. Sam

I am fun to be around because I love sports and I love to play. I am good with kids, big and small. And I love your class.

I would like to be a bird.

I like this because I had been asking to do English for one year so I am happy you came.

True sentence: My name is Sam and I love football. This is a sentence because it has a verb and a noun.

9. BD

I am 17 years old. My favourite colour is purple and I loved to play football. In the next five years after achieving my CXC passing I would like to be playing national football.

I would choose an eagle because it is the only bird that flies so high and can stay flying for a long time. That's just how I am. I have a lot of endurance and I see myself at a higher level than everybody.

I would love to be part of this class because I love to read and write and would love to learn more about it. So I include myself in this class to be certified in English.

One true sentence: I am a very strong boy.

10. Peter

My hobby is football and cricket. I am kind and fair.

(Did not choose an animal)

I want to take this class because I want to be somebody in life and to my understanding if you want to be somebody in life you have to get an education.

One true sentence: I love football.

11. Jason

I love to take a stroll in the park on evenings. I love ice cream. I love good friends who look out for you. I love God. I love English. I love football. I love fruits. I love animals.

I would like to be an eagle. I would like to be that animal because I want to soar above all obstacles.

I want to take this class because I love English and I would like to learn more.

I love football. It is true because I don't love if for the sport but love it from my heart.

12. Kan

(Wrote nothing about himself)

I would choose to be a "dog" because of the freedom it has.

I want to take this class because it is my best subject and I never got to do it in school because I got locked up.

One true sentence: I love football. It is true because I play that sport.

13. KS

I am 19 years. I love English but at times I get frustrated while doing it.

I choose to be a lion because of the powerful paws on the way it strides through the jungle and hunts down its prey.

I want to take this class because I want to learn more about English and achieve a certificate for doing it.

One true sentence: I want to be a scholar because being a scholar could help me get a good job.

14. JW

I am a footballer for YTC and I used to play with fire out in the free world. I also like women lots of women. And finally I like to pray.

I would like to be a lion because it is the most respectful animal in the jungle and it is fearless and NO animal disrespects the lion.

Because I am willing to do English and I will like to complete the English so I can get passes and achieve something very good. If I put my mind I can pass in Jesus name I could pass.

One true sentence: I like to be honest because I like people to be honest.

15. Vaughn

I am 19. I enjoy doing art work, playing basketball and swimming. I also like meeting new people and making friends.

A lion is very quiet and fast, full of patience. And very powerful. I would like to be a lion because I'll feel very soft.

This class might help me to better my reading and spelling also it might better me on my return into society.

Write one true sentence: I enjoy being in classes.

16. TS

I love cooking, cycling, playing football, school and family.

I would like to be an eagle because God made them kings of the sky because they have wings to fly and they rule over all birds in the sky.

The reason why I had joined the class is because I wanted to know how it feels to do CXC English because I had no time to do it on the outside.

The first time I came to YTC I had an infection in my left knee and I had to go for an operation to take it out, and I was successful doing it. It is true because I can tell a story about it.

17. Lal

My name is Lal and I am 18 years old. I have some goals in life. The first one is I would like to be an electrician and number two is I would to be a great football player and I would like to be a motivational speaker to help people. But first and foremost I must become a changed person so that I can be able to change people.

I do not have an animal I would like to be because God made me somebody special and I would like to be myself so that I can help people for that greater good.

I want to take this class because I would like to show people that I am not illiterate and prove to myself that I can be somebody and I will like to go back there with something rather than nothing.

One true sentence: I believe in God and this is true because God said who so ever believe in me shall not perish but have everlasting life.

18. Ashton

Ashton is a very nice person to those who really get to know him. I must admit that I am a bit of a challenge managing my anger. However I have been successfully dealing with it.

Given the opportunity to choose which animal I could be, I would certainly choose a lion. It's fast, larger than most animals in its kingdom, determined at getting what its eyes are on, and it's king in its kingdom.

I am really interested in being in this class because for many years I have run from English and Maths classes, and now that I realise my need to be educated I'm now ready to face it.

One true sentence: I love humans.

Fifteen of the original 27 students wanted to be birds, I noted as I whittled away at the list. I managed to get the class down to 19 students because of the assessment.

Eight students – most of whom wanted to be birds – needed serious remedial help at an elementary school level, as most of the lads do in YTC. That's why there's an elementary school, but no real secondary school. These eight students would not be ready for secondary school for some time. There just aren't more than a dozen young men between the ages of 15 and 18 who are truly at a secondary school level academically speaking.

I know it is unfair to keep students who need remedial help, but still it's painful to let go of boys who are begging for a chance.

In the quiet of the pitch-black night, I curled up on the couch and listened to my two pitbulls, Rambo and Duchess, snoring away.

I still had to cut more students and I had no idea how to decide which students could remain in class.

Maybe I can figure out a way to keep 17 students, I thought. Maybe I can persuade Ms McDonald. Then came the sinking feeling: If I did keep 17, I would have to figure out how to buy textbooks for all of those students. I thought: Where am I going to find the money for that?

The Forgotten Boys of Trinidad

I lost Jahmai by my third week of teaching CXC English language at YTC.

"Jahmai won't be back until further notice, but he sent work for you. He's in lockdown for fighting," the boys in my class said. (Lockdown is the YTC equivalent of solitary confinement.)

I knew I would not miss Jahmai. I had him pegged as the one boy who might give me trouble in class because of the way he muttered inaudible comments through his mouth full of gold teeth. When I say a mouth full of gold teeth, I mean every single tooth. For me, Jahmai's absence meant one less student I had to think about cutting from my class that was already too large. I was willing to write him off, and if I had succeeded in doing that, it would have been the biggest mistake I made that year.

The week Jahmai vanished from class I learned what it meant to be humble as Louis Moore, the guidance counselor in my school, sent out an e-mail asking teachers if they would like to help me buy textbooks. I managed to buy textbooks for all 17 students in my class and other supplies as well. Over time, those teachers' generosity – along with the kindheartedness of parents, principals and students – would add up to over $15,000 worth of textbooks and novels for my students. I had never felt that level of community spirit and my community of supporters would only grow over the next year.

My students accepted their books like boys getting new toy planes. They carefully placed their books on the corners of their desks and then put a hand on top of their books as though they were preventing them from flying away. Every time they glanced at their books they smiled.

I guessed that books were special because a sign on the front gate warns there is a $1,000 fine for bringing books into YTC. That is to prevent inappropriate reading material from entering the facility.

That was the good news. The bad news was the deadline looming over my head. I had to submit names for the CXC English language exam by October. I tried to submit everyone's name.

"That can't happen," said Ms McDonald, the guard in charge of post primary school classes.

Ms McDonald insisted one name had to be on that list: Jahmai.

"Don't forget Jahmai," she said.

I had planned to leave Jahmai off the list. "Write him encouraging notes. He's a boy who's always in trouble, but there is something very likeable about him," said Ms McDonald.

Jahmai couldn't walk five steps without getting in a fight, but Ms McDonald was determined to save Jahmai. She would not give up on Jahmai. In time, I too would see Jahmai's great gifts. He would keep me going through my toughest times when I would secretly sob myself to sleep after Saturday night classes.

For two months, I taught Jahmai in lockdown where he had spent the better part of two years. We never saw each other or spoke to each other while Jahmai stayed in lockdown. He sent essays through classmates – and a message not to send him any more dog books. Every time he came out, he managed to get into another fight. Back inside he would go.

Each essay Jahmai wrote had the most delicate and exquisite handwriting I had ever seen. Every assignment looked like a work of art with impeccable penmanship, clear and easy to read. His handwriting seemed somehow to help his thoughts to flow across the paper. I looked forward to Jahmai's work just to see his handwriting. Jahmai had so many interesting thoughts.

Jahmai began to send notes at the bottom of his essays. The first read, "Miss, I am always so angry, and I don't know why."

"Read," I wrote back to him, "and write. You will find people in books who share your struggles. Writing will help you to find the answers you're looking for in life."

Jahmai turned in many book reviews. He followed all my instructions – without ever seeing me – and quickly cleaned up minor problems he had with structure and writing. I only had to tell him what to do once. He never made the same mistake twice.

He read *Miguel Street* by V.S. Naipaul; classics like *The Lost World* by Jules Verne, *King Solomon's Mines* by H. Rider Hagard, *Jane Eyre* by Charlotte Bronte and the *Iliad* by Homer. He loved Greek mythology and *Water for Elephants* by Sarah Gruen would turn out to be one of his favourite books.

I soon realised Jahmai might just be one of the smartest boys I had ever taught, and I desperately wanted him back in my class.

Every week I asked, "Did Jahmai get out of lockdown?"

Ms McDonald would say, "Yes, but as soon as he got out, he got in a fight again."

One day after I left class, I spotted Jahmai in a group of boys being taken back to their dorms.

He beamed that golden smile, but this time it seemed warm and kind – not flippant or sarcastic. He seemed to be glad to see me.

"Jahmai," I called, "Do what you have to do to get back into class. Do you know what that is?" I asked.

"Yes, Miss," he smiled and then shuffled off. All those gold teeth I thought. They seemed to gleam even in the dim light.

Jahmai in Lockdown

As I tried to make the class even smaller, I worked as hard as I could every Saturday and Sunday night to keep Jahmai, who was still confined to lockdown. The irony didn't escape me. There I was agonising over how to keep a student who couldn't be in class, while some of the students sitting in front of me every Saturday would have to be cut. I wrote a letter to Jahmai.

> *Dear Jahmai,*
>
> *I am anxiously waiting for the day that you return to class. You have a place here in our class, and I am not giving it up. In the meantime, keep doing your homework, please, and keep reading.*
>
> *The more you read, the better. It will help to build the comprehension and analytical skills you need to do well on the exam.*
>
> *Study the grammar book I gave you all to share in your dorms, and work on your vocabulary. I'm giving you my copy of* The Odious Ogre *by Norton Juster and Jules Feiffer. It's a children's book, but it has really good vocabulary words.*
>
> *Make sure you understand subject/verb agreement, parallel structure, and subject/pronoun agreement – anything you can study from that reference book.*
>
> *Do any exercises you can in your textbook and I will mark them for you.*
>
> *I am sending some classics for you. Read them for pleasure and then to build your vocabulary. Study*

them for writing skills. I am sure that you can handle classics, that's why I'm sending them.

Keep sending your work, Jahmai, and write, write, write. Write essays about the books you're reading. Analyse characters.

Write about yourself too. It will help you to understand things about yourself that are below the surface and you might not realise. Write poetry. Write anything.

There is a way for things to change. You're bright, and you will figure it out. I really believe that.

Sincerely,
Miss

Jahmai answered my letter with two book reports. He rewrote them, corrected the grammatical errors I pointed out and played with punctuation in a sophisticated way.

Months later, I discovered the real meaning of those book reports for Jahmai.

Book Report: Tsotsi

By Athol Fugard

Tsotsi *is a story about faith and hardship. As well as the name of the book, Tsotsi was the main character's name. Tsotsi was faced with one of the most unbearable troubles of life, financial trouble. He was forced to live a today for today life, also he had to live by himself because he had no family. To survive he chose a life of crime because he was not a social person and he was uneducated. Faith finally struck him when he met Boston also when he was forced to be the owner of a baby.*

Growing up from birth to the age of ten, Tsotsi was loved and protected by his mother until one night the police entered his home, taking away all his hope, his mother. There on after he was adopted by a street gang of other hopeless cases like himself. To get food these boys would go around begging. As Tsotsi grew older, he changed from gang to gang until he started forming his own gang. By this time he had committed murder, rape and robbery, becoming amazingly feared in his community.

Boston was a member of Tsotsi's last gang. He was extremely well educated and he allowed nothing to stop him from speaking his mind. Tsotsi, not being one made of a lot of conversation, was angered by Boston's comments and questions about his life mainly because he did not know the answers to them. The day had come when Tsotsi had taken enough: Boston was making comment after comment about him, causing memories of Tstosi's beloved past to be triggered.

Not knowing how to balance his mixed emotions, he tried to kill Boston, almost succeeding, and then ran off confused by this renewed emotion of love.

When he had finished running, he ended up in somewhat of a forested area where he saw a young woman running and holding a box in her hand. He was in for another surprise from faith. Tsotsi snatched the woman and was about to rape her when the lid of the box fell off revealing a baby. This caused him to enter a trance just looking at it and the next thing you know, when he shook out of the trance, the woman was already gone, leaving the baby with him.

This experience combined with Boston's words caused a dramatic change in Tsotsi's behaviour: he had lost all zeal for negative things with the learning experience of raising his baby and Boston's words that kept playing over in his head, giving him a perfect memory of his childhood; reviving the feeling of love and happiness, he was on his way to fully change when he and the baby were killed after a concrete wall fell atop them in an abandoned house.

Tsotsi's entire life was driven by his hidden emotions, but it was only when he was allowed by faith to remember what love truly is that he started seeking new things in a positive manner. It is truly a pity that faith did not strike earlier.

Jahmai

In the same week, Jahmai submitted a book report on *King Solomon's Mines* by Henry Rider Haggard.

King Solomon's Mines *is a book that brings one to the understanding of how one can achieve goals. Achieving goals gives a feeling of self-satisfaction; also, to achieve goals requires strategic planning and persistence. Mr Quatermain, Sir Henry and Captain Good knew that they would require a great amount of both to accomplish the mission they set off upon. The story of their adventure to King Solomon's Mines is a narrative one, told by Quatermain. Guaranteed success will be the reward for anyone, once everyone follows effective strategic planning and remains determined all the way.*

Sir Henry and Captain Good are friends; it was on a boat trip they were fortunate to meet Quatermain. Quatermain would soon be the man to lead them to King Solomon's Mines – not for the sake of treasure – but in search of Henry's brother, George. With knowledge of the routes of the mines, Quatermain informed them that no one had ever made it to the mines and lived to tell the tale.

Determined to find his brother, Henry promised him anything money could buy – within reason – or even money itself to still carry them to the mines. Quatermain, who stood old in age, but still strong enough to move around effectively, agreed to this: He would be the boss of the journey, with the power to turn back if he so desired. Money in the sum of 1000 pounds would be paid to his son, to ensure he finished medical school and 200 pounds for himself before their trip. Last he stated that all treasure – once found – be split between himself and Good.

Knowing the hazards that lay ahead, he took his time in assembling all the needed items for the trip, bearing in mind, too heavy a load would only tire them faster. He bought a strong carriage, 20 oxen – 15 would have been enough, but he knew that even those great beasts would suffer injuries – some medicine and his weapons.

Before he left he needed only one more thing, some trustworthy and brave men besides Henry and Good. So in addition he took a tracker, a leader for the oxen driver and Umbopa, a friend of Quatermain's, a long time ago. Umbopa knowing of the defeat of men who dared to seek the mines, implied that the man who they were about to seek would probably already be dead. This only increased the determination of Henry to get confirmation about his brother's fate.

The journey started off smoothly until they began to cross the desert where they were forced to continue on foot. It was only then that the journey had started coughing up its bitter contents, resulting in the deaths of all the newly added African soldiers except Umbopa. Hunger, thirst, as well as the climate almost claimed their lives. It was thanks to the wits of Quatermain their lives were spared. They asked the tribe leader about King Solomon's Mines and he knew exactly where it was and would soon take them there after they had met the king of their tribe.

It was at the tribe's village after meeting the king that they saw and heard from the villagers how evil he was; how he became heir of the throne. By then, many encounters with death had faced them, and they started to believe that Henry's brother could not have survived it all. Now they had decided to help wage war upon the king, with some of the warriors of the village so that Umbopa would have gained the throne and become king. Timid as Quatermain was inside, he acted out of bravery on the outside, downing men as he supported Umbopa to gain the throne.

Man after Man the king and all who supported him in battle were killed and Umbopa was crowned king. Fate had it that they put aside their own goal for awhile, but they were back on track because determination burned within them still even though they already presumed Henry's brother was dead.

There on after, support was given to them in full by the tribe's men as they continued on to the mines being led directly by an old witch doctoress of the village. At last they made it to the mines where they discovered the treasure. Rejoicing in their finds, the witch slipped out from their presence and trapped them inside the mines but died in doing so.

Destined for doom now at this point, their spirits of hope were broken down but persistence still had not left them. After using all the clues given to them, they made their way out and returned to the village in high spirits because escaping the mines alive had become one of their goals. After saying goodbye to Umbopa and the villagers, they were granted escorts to take them back using an easier route to return to where they originally started. It was here they found Henry's brother alive and took him back with them.

The journey to the mines had in the past devoured all who dared travel along its path. However, with proper preparation, intelligence and persistence nothing is unachievable. What had happened along their journey was fate had required them to go out of their way for a while but they still did not lose track of their initial goal. They were satisfied with themselves because they had achieved what no man, to their knowledge, had ever achieved.

Jahmai

Jahmai always answered my letters with a book report. I thought the book reports showed a sign of respect and appreciation for bringing books to him. Some day he would tell me, "Books gave me freedom in YTC. I travelled to Africa and went along for the adventures of *King Solomon's Mines*. I experienced love in *Water for Elephants*. I was there with the ancient Greek right alongside Orpheus when he went to Hades to get back Eurydice."

At the time, I realised books meant more than a means of escape for Jahmai. He could meet new people and work out his feelings with characters in a book like *Tsotsi*. Books meant the world to Jahmai, and I still did not understand or know why he gravitated towards classics. I would be surprised which classic Jahmai would choose as his favourite read and what he would tell me some day about why he loved classics.

Looking back on those book reports I realise how much passive voice Jahmai and most of the boys used when they wrote. Life was something that happened to them and their writing reflected that.

After two months in lockdown, Jahmai came back to class. He would learn to express his feelings and fears through writing. He would analyse characters as though he were peeling off the layers of an onion.

He would not get into another fight that year. Jahmai turned out to be a pillar on which I built my English class. He would give me great insights into the forgotten boys of Trinidad. He would teach me about faith, perseverance and acceptance. Jahmai would give me the gift of hope.

A Rainy Day

I waited for the rain to subside when I reached YTC. A mother and her daughter passed me as they came out of the visitor's gate. They waited for a glimpse of one of the lads. The teenager emerged from the visitor's room and walked slowly behind the guard. He glanced over his shoulder as he walked across the grounds, and the mother smiled and waved until he disappeared behind a building. I think she was crying.

I unloaded two boxes of books at the YTC gate, and then wondered how I would get them across the field to the library. The guards called two students from class.

I said, "Why don't we leave the books here and come back for them after the rain stops?"

"Miss, we'll get plastic bags and cover them. We'll take them now," they said.

They would not leave the books behind.

When I got to the library, a guard had several lads watching a movie. The guard asked if we could go to a classroom instead of having class in the library. That upset me because I came at 4:00 p.m. so that we could have a decent place for class.

I said, "Well, I want the library, but I'll leave it up to my students. They can decide. I think we should stay."

The students said, "Miss, we'll get you the Life Skills room. It's air conditioned."

I agreed, not knowing what I was agreeing to. Seventeen of us piled in a small, freezing room meant for about eight students. "Is it too cold for you, Miss?" they asked. It was freezing. They organised to turn down the air conditioning.

My students manoeuvered themselves between the tightly packed desks. Eventually I realised that they didn't want to box me in the corner, so I moved the desk so that I could barely get to the white board, but they'd have more room.

Some students, including Olton, didn't show up for class because of a rugby match.

The nurse set up a table just outside the classroom and most of the boys pushed their way out of the room to get to the nurse.

"What are they doing?" I asked.

Marc, who's always so serious shook his head and said, "They're going to see if they can get a Motrin or something – anything to kill the pain."

"What pain?" I asked.

He shrugged. "Any pain," he said. "Most of them don't even have any real pain."

Passing out books felt like passing out candy. Marc wanted some of the books and I said, "None of these are for you —"

He said with disappointment, "because I already have books."

I said, "No, because I have Maya Angelou for you." He had asked me for books by Maya Angelou.

I sat at my desk and held up Marc's books: *I Know Why the Caged Bird Sings*, *All God's Children Need Traveling Shoes*, and *Wouldn't Take Nothing for My Journey Now*. With his mouth wide open, Marc stared in a combination of awe and shock. He stood to receive the books and said, "Thank you, Miss. I can't believe it."

As usual, they stacked the books neatly on the corner of their desks, and touched them during the class. They kept organising them, pressing them into shape as people do when they're trying to neatly stack a pile of papers.

Eventually, the class became so crowded they couldn't put another chair in the room. Four boys squeezed in the room after going to the nurse and stood sideways for two and a half hours.

We discussed an article about an American football player who died falling out of the back of a truck after he had a fight with his girlfriend. He tumbled out of the van after she sped off. The article had a problem with subject/antecedent agreement so we used it for a grammar exercise as well as a lesson on ignorance.

If we hadn't been packed in a room like sardines, it would have been almost cozy sitting there with the rain tapping against the roof.

On the other hand, there were many evenings of shouting above the rain pelting the galvanized iron roof like bullets. One day there was so much rain that YTC flooded.

Kheelon came back from the bathroom with disturbing news: "Miss, it's going to flood out there. I think you should go home."

"How can you send Miss out in that rain?" Marc shouted. Some students thought I should make a break for it. "It will only get worse," they kept saying. Some said to stay. I decided to stay, and I was stranded in YTC.

"You're going to have to sleep in here tonight," the boys laughed.

When class finished, and I walked to my car, which I had parked inside the compound for once, police helicopters hovered over YTC and prison row that stretched out along the road: Golden Grove, Maximum Security Prison, a Women's Prison.

Cars had drifted along the flooded road like toy boats on a lake. Some floated off the roadway and into a ditch. Others washed into the road that turns into YTC. Nervous about the rising water and the thought of caimans, Trinidad's version of alligators, that I knew had spilled out of the lake in the back of

YTC and into the river the rain had just made, I fidgeted and sighed. The road had vanished, and we were cut off from the main guard booth at the entrance of YTC.

It was almost 7:30 p.m. Sensing my discomfort, Mr Sterling Stewart, the supervisor of YTC, said, "Do you want to go back by your boys?"

"Yes," I said. I went back into the school after lockdown and waited for the rain to stop. Marc, Jahmai, Kheelon, Peter, Ashton, Shawn and a few other boys came back to sit with me.

In YTC, the boys already had told me, you have to take advantage of the little things: a walk across the grounds to help someone carry a box; an errand to the Administration building, but this was something big – like breaking curfew. My students were out of the dorms after 7:00 p.m. lockdown, and that was a rare feat. It gave them a sense of power in a place where any semblance of power is stripped away the minute they enter those creaking gates.

The boys kept idle chatter going to keep my mind off the possibility of staying in YTC for the night. It was the first time they were in a position to take care of me. Over time I would realise just how much they relished the nurturing role. It was totally incongruous with the tough boy image that had once defined their lives. I left YTC at about 9:30 p.m.

The Pen is Mightier than the Sword

Still trying to narrow down my class, I began to give more short, in-class assignments to see if any of the boys who weren't handing in homework could handle the CXC-level work. It could be, I tried to convince myself, that some students weren't submitting work because they lacked the confidence to complete an assignment. I could imagine a capable student hiding in class behind his poor self-esteem. I searched desperately for that student, but didn't seem to be discovering him. Deep down, I knew I had to deal with those who just wouldn't perform. There had to be a certain level of discipline to pull off this decision to fast-track this class. This was a sprint, not a marathon. I had begun to warn my students, "If you don't hand in work, I can't keep you in class." They showed no emotion. With all of this in mind, I gave an assignment. Write a paragraph analysing this statement: "The pen is mightier than the sword." Explain what that means in one paragraph.

"What does it mean?" they asked.
"You tell me," I said. "Figure it out."
Here's what they wrote:

Marc Friday:

The pen mightn't be as deadly as a razor-sharp sword but trust me, the famous quote, "The pen is mightier than the sword" is as true as it gets. In that one statement we see many different views on life. The pen could be David and the sword could be Goliath. We all know what took place there. Small things or good things always are used to show the strength of a people, in this case, "the pen".

(No name)

The pen is very powerful. It depends on how you use it. The sword is also powerful when you use it physically. The difference is you can express yourself without anyone getting hurt using the pen.   You can write something like history on paper and someone in the future can read it. I want to give you my view – when you kill someone with a sword you'll go for trial and the pen will sentence you.

Jahmai:

Honestly I have never heard the quote "the pen is mightier than the sword," but by just thinking about it, I am convinced already. The pen, I believe, symbolises education and the sword, weapons of destruction. Both items can bring about many different forms of power to the beholder but one also comes with a tremendous amount of negative consequences. The sword is meant to bring control to law breakers but it is the pen that makes the law. The pen is the backbone for any great ruler. Any unlawful sword will be put to an end by the sword of justice, which is the sword of the pen.

Daniel:

I think that the pen is mightier than the sword because the pen has more uses. With the pen you can write and send letters. You can do important things like school work, and that can help you reach far in life. With the sword, you can cut things and use it for crime. The pen is very powerful for plenty people because the pen carries them the distance they want to go. To me, that is why the pen is mightier than the sword.

Christian:

The pen could write on until the ink runs out and it could kill and write about the death. The pen has a big difference from a sword. The sword can't write but it could kill. The pen has power in it to write a sentence, and it could make money.

Brandon:

The pen is mightier than the sword because the pen will give you knowledge and life.

Kheelon:

The pen is mightier than the sword because of what the pen can do that the sword can't do. For example, you can kill a man with the sword, but you can do mightier things with the pen and you can do things that mean a lot to people, like write a letter. Letters means a lot to people.

Kern:

The pen is mightier than the sword is an adage, which has two or more meanings, but the most common meaning is this: by using the sword, you are engaging in violence where you might end up dead or tied up with the law, and by using the pen you most likely become someone positive in life like: a doctor, a lawyer, a teacher or a prime minister.

Stephen:

Some say that the sword is stronger than the pen, but to me it's the other way around. You see the sword leaves marks on the outside, but a pen leaves marks on the inside. So put down the swords and learn to use a pen and you will know something on the inside, not the outside.

Jean Pierre:

The pen is powerful because writing is better than doing evil things. Instead of doing wrong, you can write down your feelings. Instead of going outside and doing something negative, you can stay inside and write something.

Ashton:

In terms of being used to do immediate, grievous bodily harm, this phrase can easily be untrue because of the sword's abilities to chop and slice, however, if one realistically examines the abilities of the pen, one would recognise that while the sword can be used to commit a greater, physical bodily harm immediately, the pen has the ability to write the spoken word and also show our most heinous thoughts which if written, read and executed properly can cause harm, not only physically but mentally and emotionally. Billions of people can be killed by bearing in mind the power of words.

"Were we right?" they asked as I glanced over their answers.

"There's hardly ever a wrong or right answer when it comes to constructing an argument in English," I said. "You make your own argument and defend it."

A room of smiles popped up in front of me. Encouraged, I returned their smiles.

Biting the Bullet

I knew that only about six of my students were truly CXC-level students – and I knew I wasn't giving up Olton, the 17-year-old who wanted to be a turtle.

"Are you sure?" Ms McDonald said when I told her I couldn't give up Olton. "I know he's one of the weaker ones."

Olton's one paragraph on why he wanted to be a turtle showed me so much: creativity, compassion, empathy; the ability to form an argument. I had to have Olton.

"Yes," I said. "I am certain of Olton. I know he's weak, but he tries hard. That's all I need."

I believed in Olton with all my heart, and I hoped he wouldn't let me down. I would feel awful to know I might have given Olton a place that a stronger student could have filled, and to tell you the truth, almost any student seemed to be stronger than Olton. But I would not let go. Ms McDonald knew that and so she finally shrugged and said, "Your call, but da'ling (she called everyone da'ling) you have to get that class down."

"I will," I promised, and then put it out of my mind.

I headed for class with a plan to cover everything in all the CXC English textbooks we could find. In the first class that I had handed out the textbooks, we tackled grammar so I could get a feel for how much grammar they knew.

Now, we were going to tackle reading passages. I'm not a textbook person, but I decided to grin and bear it for the sake of the exam.

"We'll begin with the poem 'Blackberry Picking' by Seamus Heaney," I said to my students.

They smiled, nodded and shuffled around in their chairs. This is weird, I thought. They're far too excited about a poem about blackberry picking.

One of the students read, "Where briars scratched and wet grass bleached our boots. Round hayfields, cornfields and potato-drills/We trekked and picked until the cans were full… Our hands were peppered/With thorn pricks, our palms sticky as Bluebeard's…"

The more they read, the more I wanted to crawl into a hole. When they finished reading, there was dead silence.

My students stared at me in utter dismay. It seemed as though they had been collectively slapped in the face. Clearly this could not be a poem about Blackberry cell phones as they had originally expected.

"I find that poem deeply disturbing," I said, and they laughed.

Marc asked, "Did this guy make up his name?"

"He's Irish," I said.

"Oh," said Marc, like that explained everything.

And then came the questions: "What's a blackberry?" "What's a thorn?"

I fumbled around trying to explain what blackberries were and that thorns were picka. I felt like a fool – but this was the textbook.

Once they knew that Bluebeard was a pirate, they said, "Ohhh, I get it. He's taking the blackberries like a thief because a pirate is like a thief."

Oh boy, I thought, I have to get something out of this class other than possible CXC passes earned from wading through boring textbooks filled with irrelevant material. I have to get something meaningful for them to read, something they can relate to and something that will teach them some thinking skills for life. Not much of that, if anything, would be found in that textbook.

It was a real dilemma. We needed the textbooks so they could get used to some of the boring passages they would get on a test, but many of the passages were just plain useless. I would have to come up with my own material from the Internet.

But would I be able to get away with this? Would I be able to prepare them for the exam if I strayed from the textbook? Was I cheating them and hurting their chances if I went down my own path? My biggest fear came from not knowing how far I could stray from the norm. The journalist in me is always looking for an exciting read. I felt very uneasy. I didn't know what to do, and I didn't have the confidence to follow my heart.

Living with Fear

With every passing week I felt more and more frightened and too embarrassed to go back to YTC to teach CXC English language. My students weren't the problem. If they had misbehaved or wasted a minute of my time, the decision to leave YTC would have been easy. But they were the perfect class. Still, something felt wrong, and I couldn't quite put my finger on it.

My own indecisiveness bothered me. I couldn't decide which students to give up. In time, that problem would take care of itself. Some students got shifted to work programmes. Some never turned in any homework so it didn't seem feasible to keep them. Some needed remedial work, and in all fairness I had to point them in the right direction if they weren't ready for CXC English language exams.

I found it disconcerting that I knew nothing about my students, but then I didn't want to know anything about them or their troubled past. I knew that everyone in YTC was in some kind of trouble, and many boys had committed crimes that were far worse than I could imagine. In time they would share snippets of the anger, violence and chaos that had defined their lives. Some of those stories would knock the wind out of me.

I lost two students indefinitely.

"They had a fight and they're in lockdown," the class said nonchalantly. Fights seem to be an everyday occurrence.

"They're doing their homework, though, Miss, and they asked us to collect the work for them," the boys said.

"They won't be back until further notice," the boys told me.

I am ashamed to say I still thought about quitting in spite of the fact my colleagues had already given me money to buy books.

While fumbling for a reason to quit, I called Sgt. Roger Alexander of Crime Watch fame. (I knew Alexander long before he became a star on Ian Alleyne's TV show because he had got my stolen dog, Jada, back for me four years ago.) A big, rough cop with a hearty laugh and a deep, fearless voice, Alexander raided the communities these lads came from.

"I don't know if I should go on teaching these boys," I said to Alexander, hoping he'd give me a way out.

"Nah," Alexander said emphatically. "Keep going. It's a good thing. They're boys. They can change. Education is important."

I couldn't face the textbooks any more. Too routine. Too boring. Too dry. Too irrelevant for boys who wanted English for real life. There was no way getting around that.

The next week, Ms McDonald called me at work.

"Decision time. Call names," she said. "You have to choose."

I frantically flipped through those initial assessments. I called every name.

"Nah, nah. You can't call all."

I felt myself shaking. I didn't want to make the decision.

Ms McDonald started going down the list and calling names, and the ones I could imagine – the ones who handed in work and participated in class made the list. We both agreed on who would sit the exam, and who would remain in class even though he wouldn't sit the exam.

"I'm still not sure about Olton," Ms McDonald said.

"I am." I was willing to fight to the end for Olton.

When I hung up the phone, I looked at the names in front of me and sighed. I would not agonise over who to keep again. I reminded myself that many lads came to class, but didn't hand in any work. It should have been easy to cut them, but it wasn't. Still, this list felt right. Out of 180 boys in YTC I had a class of eight English students. I struck a compromise with YTC: Kheelon would sit the exam even though it was doubtful that he would be ready. Another student, Vaughn, would not be taking the exam, but he would remain with me because he had never missed a single class. Vaughn's tenacity had been the deciding factor. Much to my surprise, Ms McDonald supported my decision to keep Vaughn. Strange, I thought, that YTC so readily agreed for me to keep a student who could not take the exam. Months later, I would find out why that decision to keep Vaughn had made everyone in YTC happy.

This was my list:

1. Jahmai – Determined to make an impression and bury the image of the Trinidad "rude" boy with the gold teeth and a brazen attitude, Jahmai now wanted to prove everyone in YTC wrong. "I am not a waste of time," he said. He would fight the reputation he had built as a scrappy, belligerent young man with a short fuse. "I know my heart, and I am not evil," he said. He was determined to find out why he felt so angry.

2. Shawn – Street-smart, suave and business-like, Shawn, a promising footballer with a no-nonsense attitude, knew how to play the academic game. His just-show-me-how-to-do-it attitude served him well. He loved structure and he cranked out cookie-cutter essays. He worked the façade of being tough like a model works a runway. "I have a reputation for being tough in here," he told me. He advised me in a kind, gentle, non-threatening way not to blow his cover.

3. Ashton – Smooth-talking Ashton, the go-to man in YTC, developed a reputation as a role model for YTC's

mentoring programme. He reminded me of Red in *The Shawshank Redemption*. If someone blindfolded you and dropped you from a helicopter into that prison, you would know where you had landed because the first sound you would hear would undoubtedly be a chorus of people calling Ashton's name. Ashton, the master organiser; Ashton, the charming leader of YTC, knew how to motivate everyone. Now, he wanted to write as well as he could speak.

4. Peter – The roughest of the lot, distant, guarded and quiet to the point of almost being invisible, Peter was determined to never let his guard down and never become too close to anyone. He had to move around to learn. Don't tie him down, don't push him emotionally, and he would deliver amazing work. In time, he would smile, and open up more.

5. Kheelon – A natural athlete, Kheelon, another promising footballer, was a weak, but fearless student. He spoke and wrote only in Creole. His writing had good structure. He struggled with grammar, but knocked out two-page essays. Brave, funny and always willing to tackle a problem, Kheelon was not nearly ready to take an English exam in eight months, but his determination and his endearing personality won me over. It's rare to find a weak student who is unafraid to write, and that earned Kheelon a spot in class, and a chance to take the CXC English language exam. YTC and I decided to gamble on Kheelon.

6. Marc – Bubbly, determined and always singing, Marc possessed the best creative writing skills. My challenge was to get Marc to write mundane things like summaries. Marc could spark discussions and provoke responses from students. His life, opinions and emotions were like an open book. He never tried to gloss over any problem or issue. He simply had to express himself.

7. Olton – Although he was a weak student not yet ready for CXC English, my rugby player, Olton, who would earn a spot on the Under-19 National Rugby team of Trinidad and Tobago, had impressed me with that one paragraph he wrote about wanting to be a turtle. His optimism and humour made him special. A dreamy soul, Olton always talked about the future with a wife and kids. A stocky teen with a deep, crackling voice, Olton managed to soften the edges so that he always sounded polite. Olton epitomised sheer will power.

8. Vaughn – Quietly determined, Vaughn did not feel ready for the CXC exam, but he did his work and silently convinced me to keep him in class. There was something admirable about his determination. I didn't know quite why I wanted to keep him even though we all agreed he would not take the exam. I had a gut feeling that he should be there. Perhaps it's because he was always waiting for me when I came to class. He was always the first one there.

I had my class. Everything was settled. Now, I needed to figure out a plan on my own terms because I wasn't going to sell my soul – my teaching soul – to teach CXC English language in YTC.

Friday

Walking across the eerily quiet, water-logged grounds of YTC made me feel like Robinson Crusoe shipwrecked on a deserted island. People coming from other programmes inside the facility passed me like ships in the night. The guard sitting in the back of my classroom seemed surreal, like someone on a distant shore. My own students, who faithfully attended English class, felt more like apparitions than young men. They were distant and reluctant to trust anyone. But I had Friday.

Friday asked for lots of poetry and lots of Shakespeare to read.

Friday wrote about his life:

> *My mother and father were poor people; therefore, I too was poor. My mother was an explorer and she loved to travel – I think that's where I got my liking for adventure. My life has been an exciting adventure. In 1994 I was carried away to England but because of my troublesome ways I was sent back to Trinidad and Tobago. When I returned in the year 2000, I was hailed as the prodigal son. My favour was lost and soon after I fell into a trap.*
>
> *I made a critical decision in my life at age twelve that would eventually change my life forever. This decision took me on a trip that I would love, but also regret. Crime and jail were an inevitable part of the road I chose. I could never say that it was not my fault. I would never dare blame my parents – they weren't around enough to blame. It was my fault*

entirely. Maybe I was led astray or maybe I was just stupid. I might take a while to figure that out, but until then let's say my life was the most extraordinary expedition anyone could endure.

Like all writers, Friday would fight loneliness:

Sometimes I sit – either by myself or in a crowd – and my mind goes places too far to carry anyone else. Maybe if I could carry at least one person he might like it. Words could never completely express my thoughts or feelings. I tried to tell a friend (friend is so uncomfortable to say) how I was feeling once and he thought I was mad. Maybe I am.

Tears fail to come to my eyes sometimes. I want them to, but maybe they're all dried up and have become sodium chlorine crystals in my eyes. They might fall and one day hopefully unclog the passage way. I wish they would.

There are a lot of things to cry about inside this big caged 'place'. It's not so bad, but sometimes it bites hard. I can't remember the last time I heard "cockle-doodle-doo": the sound of a rooster. I mean, that's not really any big, fascinating thing, but the simplicity is the attraction. Weird huh?

I am going all over the place; so would you if you were here. My thoughts could never be entirely focused: There are so much things to think and at the same time so little. Anyway, I finally got rid of my boredom. Thank God for writing.

Friday always searched for love and acceptance. When I gave him this statement to analyse: "Not everyone is healthy enough to love you", Friday wrote:

I live in a crazy country and sometimes I love it. Then on other occasions I don't. Where I'm from it seems

*like it's forbidden to show your feelings. Like I would
be called a woman if I do or I might lose a woman
if I don't. Thanks to three years of life skills classes in
YTC, I understand now that not everybody is mentally
capable of showing love.*

Friday's classwork barely scratched the surface of his writing talent. Safely hidden inside his well-guarded notebooks were sizzling stories of his chaotic life; an epic poem about the journey of a nerd who falls from grace, and the beginning of a bittersweet novel about a strong woman who served as the spiritual centre of a poor, crime-ridden village.

A deep, dark and daring writing style, raw and honest, gave Friday his voice. Friday ambushed readers by juxtaposing soft and soulful descriptions with harsh images for breathtaking results. He knew how to pace a story, create complex characters and string together hair-raising conflicts. But Friday also had to write mundane summaries for the CXC English language exam. I tried to guide Friday in the direction of his exam. After all, I was his Crusoe.

"You have to practise writing summaries," I kept telling him.

I wanted Friday to feel success; I wanted Friday to pass his exam. I often thought: what if such a talented, young writer had to feel like a failure because of a test that could never measure his true ability?

This was my fear for Friday, and it haunted me.

Moving Right Along...

It is hard not to feel totally amazed when you show students something once and they do it without ever looking back again. So it was with writing essays. In one fell swoop, they straightened out the problems they had writing essays – namely structure – by simply following instructions.

They quickly learned the basic format of an essay: how to identify a theme, turn it into a thesis statement, answer the question why or how, provide three pieces of support and a conclusion. They learned to get out of the abstract and use examples once they had identified their support.

"That's it?" they asked as they followed each step.

"No one ever told us to do it like that," said Olton.

"The problem is you're often taught to start with an 'introduction' – and by the way you are banned from using that word in my class. It's not an introduction. It's a beginning. An introduction is talking about what you're going to talk about. It's fluff. You have to write summaries or argumentative essays and you don't have any time for fluff. Get right to the point."

Shawn cranked out endless essays.

Suddenly I realised I had more time to teach than the months showed. With attentive boys who listened well and had no discipline issues, I figured every three-hour class was worth six hours.

They loved learning about the structure of language from the syntax of a sentence to the organisation of a paragraph and essay, and they plugged into structure as though they were conforming to a new rule in YTC. Show them how to structure any type of essay and they'd crank them out like they were running a bootleg essay factory inside those dorms. I didn't have to worry about plagiarism because students had no Internet in YTC. I knew the essays they handed in were original.

I began to think of other ways to save time. What if I had someone who could teach them when I wasn't around? After all, these boys had a lot of time on their hands. Yes, YTC kept them busy, but they had no Internet or cell phone distractions. There were no girls to turn their heads; no weekend limes to think about. TV was the only distraction they had.

I would like to think I came up with the answer the moment I thought of the question, but as usual, I fumbled my way through this entire mission.

It wasn't until the boys invited me to stay for Stephen Dubay's movie night that the answer came to me. Once a month, Stephen came to YTC to beam a popular movie on a giant screen set up in the playing field.

That night, they were seeing *Karate Kid*. Some guests came to give speeches including the musicians 3canal.

"What are you doing here?" Wendell Manwarren of 3canal asked.

"I'm teaching CXC English," I said, but the voice sounded like it was coming from someone else other than me. I still had a hard time visualising myself teaching in a boys' prison.

"Is there anything you need?" he asked. "I'd like to help."

Without thinking I said, "I could use copies of *Miguel Street* for all of my students to read.

And just like that it came to me: Just as I had used Hemingway to help me through the first class, I could use our Trinidadian Nobel laureate V.S. Naipaul to help me teach tone and the beauty of writing sentences. I could give them articles from the Internet that demonstrated good writing and I'd give them all the books I could get my hands on. I began to take notes on the lads' interests so I could match reading material with boys.

I was already giving them books, but now I thought of books that would help them more with language, the structure of language, vocabulary and life skills – not just fun books to read.

Wendell stayed true to his word. He got all my students copies of *Miguel Street*, and they were pleasantly surprised – not just at the gesture, but at Naipaul.

"It's funny, Miss," they said. "It's a really funny book."

"Yes, it is," I said.

"We didn't know people wrote books that were funny," said Olton.

"People write all kinds of books. You can feel every emotion in a book. The more you read," I said, "the more you can soak in language and structure and grammar and spelling. Read for fun, and then look at the way writers craft a sentence."

So began our journey into reading not just for pleasure, but reading with a purpose: a language journey meant to be every bit as important as their classes.

Movies, I thought could have the same result. They could be a visual model for all of the literary elements and the structure of writing. What is a movie anyway, but a succession of images strung together to show a theme?

I had to go away for a week to my daughter's fashion show at the International Academy of Design and Technology in Tampa so I left the 1993 movie, *Cool Runnings*, the story of the 1988 Jamaican Olympic bobsled team, for my class to see.

I wanted to leave them with something upbeat, and something that would help motivate them and show them about theme while I was gone.

Shawn gave me an essay about *Cool Runnings* when I got back.

Cool Runnings
by Shawn

Cool Runnings *simply showed as long as you are determined and you have the will power to go forward, you can always succeed.*

Look at Derice, who was the driver for the Jamaican bobsled team. His main goal was to go to the Olympics. He tried running, but was set back. When one of the sprinters fell and tripped him in a race, it might have seemed that his life in sports was over, but it wasn't.

Then there was Derice's best friend who showed passion for another form of bobsledding, which was driving carts. Together, with a two-time gold medalist at the Olympic level who fell from glory when he put weights on the bobsled, they formed a team and set out to reach the Olympics in a winter sport not made for tropical countries.

Each individual on the team displayed strength and determination. Sanka, the rasta, had to overcome his fear of cold weather. One of the young men had problems co-operating with others. He had to put that aside for the bobsled team. The third guy came from a rich family. His father wanted the best for him. He had to go against his father's wishes and stand up to the man who made him what he was. The coach had to put aside his past, forget all the criticism and get the young men on the right track.

What I liked the most was that in the end, the bobsled, that wasn't very wholesome in the first place, gave up and overturned. The team had enough pride in their country to get up, lift the bobsled and walk to the finish line.

So, to close, you must overcome all obstacles, put differences aside, set your eyes on your goals and work for them. Also, you should never forget where you came from. Cool Runnings was a huge hit….

A couple of months into teaching, we watched Clint Eastwood's movie *Gran Torino* about an angry Korean War veteran and widower who lived in a neighbourhood overrun by gangs.

There was a rhyme and reason for watching movies namely building various literary skills, but watching movies felt like a reward as well. There's only so much grammar you can kill in three hours. Somewhere along the way someone's head is going to burst with a three-hour class and it seemed it would be mine. These boys would never say time to quit. They never gave any indication they were too tired. I had to call it a day.

Most of all, movies gave me a better insight into the way my students thought. We are shaped by our backgrounds, and the insights we have about literature come from our own experiences. We all know this. Still, their viewpoints surprised me, especially when they wrote about theme in the movie *Gran Torino*.

Olton wrote, "The main theme of the movie is caring; then love, friendship and sacrifice."

Kheelon listed the themes as love, hate, forgiveness and understanding.

Shawn said acceptance was the main theme. At the top of his essay he wrote this:

> *Mr Kowalski had to accept the people around him.*
> *He had to accept he was getting old.*
> *He had to accept he wasn't in the military anymore.*

Shawn wrote this essay:

> *Mr Kowalski was an old man who, on the surface, seemed to carry a lot of hatred: hatred for his sons, hatred for his family and most prevalent, hatred for*

his neighbours. He hated the fact that he was sick and might be dying soon. He survived the Korean War and killed 13 enemy soldiers, and now the neighbourhood in which he was living all his life was swamped by Asians – even his doctor was replaced by an Asian. He had to accept the fact that he couldn't kill any of these people because he was no longer at war so he would have to live and cope with them all.

Mr Kowalski had to accept the fact that he was getting old. We see this when he couldn't move the freezer and had to call Tao to help him. (He was sick and coughing blood and he knew he was going to die soon). He overcame everything he was in denial about. He began co-operating with all of his neighbours and became a hero, saving them and pulling them out of situations.

When the Hmong gang members struck, Mr Kowalski accepted that everyone – even the Catholic priest – was looking up to him to retaliate. He did it in a way that was contrary to what everyone was thinking. When they expected him to shoot at gang members, he ensured that they shot him and they would all be convicted of murder so he accepted that he was going to die and chose to do it in a way that would benefit his whole neighbourhood.

When my class discussed the movie they easily recognized Walt Kowalski's anger, but they didn't see it stemming from the guilt he lived with in life for killing people in the Korean War. They saw his anger coming from losing his wife and not having anyone in his life to love him.

"What is really wrong with Walt is that he has no one to love him," they all said.

"Walt genuinely liked Tao because he saw that Tao needed a chance in life because the gangs wouldn't leave him alone," said Peter, "and Walt's family was only after him for money."

When Walt was looking at the doctor's papers and talking to his son, they felt that Walt had made up his mind that he was sick, and he wouldn't waste the money to make himself better. He knew he couldn't ask his family to help him.

He wanted to make sure that Tao was safe, and he wanted to make sure that there was no way the gang would get off.

"He wanted his life to stand for something," said Olton, "and he wanted a sense of family."

"Walt had nothing to lose because he was coughing up blood," they said. "But the biggest reason why Walt decided to give up his life for Tao was that he genuinely cared about Tao because Tao was respectful so he could love him like a son."

For them, a movie like *Gran Torino* was not defined by anger or violence. They didn't find it a disturbing movie. They found it a sad movie because Walt Kowalski had no love in his life. That's what made them sad: no love in Walt's life.

Initially, they thought Walt was crazy. In the end, they liked and respected him.

In the end, my students said, "Mr Kowalski was hurt and angry because he had no one to love him. He wasn't angry and distant because he was haunted by memories of the Korean War. War was the only place he ever functioned. He felt angry and frustrated because he was living in the middle of a war zone and he couldn't operate like it was a war."

For me, movie time with my students at YTC ended up giving language, literature and life a whole new meaning.

Marley and I Fight the Battle of I

I can admit now that I thought it was a conspiracy. My students were out to drive me crazy without ever saying a word or misbehaving in class. I know that sounds paranoid, but what else could I think? There they were in the beginning – the perfect CXC English language class inside YTC. Working diligently every Saturday from 4:00 p.m. to 7:00 pm and Sunday from 1:00 p.m. to 4:00 p.m., they did everything I taught them. They wrote amazing essays with compelling and unusual arguments. They wrote complex sentences and they used sophisticated punctuation: semicolons, colons, dashes and commas. They were articulate. They could spell fairly well.

But they would not capitalise the pronoun *I*.

I was upset. "This is crazy," I told them. "You are racking up points with thesis statements that are profound and different from what anyone else would write. When you write essays, you have solid arguments to back up your unusual viewpoints, and then you're losing marks because you won't capitalise the pronoun *I*."

My students stared at me with faces that could have been blank slates.

"Why do we have to capitalise *I*?" they asked.

"Because it's a rule. Just do it," I said. "We don't have time to waste on debating a rule like capitalising the pronoun *I*."

"But if we have to capitalise the pronoun *I*, then we have to capitalise *you*, *he*, *she*…" said Kheelon.

"No, only if those pronouns are at the beginning of a sentences or if you're referring to God – the Christian one – not the Greek ones," I said.

I thought we had reached an agreement. After all, they were used to following rules. My students continued to hand in brilliant essays, and still they would not capitalise the pronoun *I*.

Remember, we were trying to get through the two-year CXC English language syllabus in eight months. I felt we were wasting time.

One class I said, "Consider this: I am important. I beat my chest like a mother gorilla. I am the most important person in the world, so the pronoun *I* is like a proper name – your own first and last names: Capitalise it."

And they said once again, "But what about *she*, *he* and *you*? They're important too."

"And *it*?" I asked.

They thought hard. "I guess," they said, "we should capitalise *it* as well."

"No!" I had totally lost my patience.

Why couldn't they see this?

The next class I devised a lesson based on "The Epistemological Significance of 'I-an-I'"…in *Chanting Down Babylon*, a collection of academic essays about Rastafarianism published by Ian Randle Publishers in Jamaica. This essay examined the role of pronouns and the built-in conditions of pronoun usage in Rastafarian English. I thought I would compare and contrast that with the use of pronouns in Jamaican Creole, Trinidad Creole and formal English. This was forcing me to dabble in the roots of my anthropological linguistics.

I told my students, "In Trinidad Creole, we don't use possessive pronouns like *my*, *your* and *our*. "We say, 'she house' or 'he car'. Jamaican Creole doesn't use subjective pronouns like *I* or *we*. Jamaicans say something like 'Me cyan explain the pronoun *I*'. Jamaicans use an objective pronoun, *me*, for the subjective pronoun *I*."

They seemed to be following what I was saying. "What does 'I an' I' mean in Rastafarian English?" I asked.

Marc was the only student who knew that 'I an' I' meant 'God an' I.'

"'I an' I' is a conscious effort to get rid of colonial baggage and give Caribbean speakers a concept of subjective *I*," I told my students.

"The importance of *I* is double because God stands beside me – *I*," said Marc.

Problem solved, I thought, as I watched my students realise the subtle message that language – even pronouns – convey important information about the way we think.

But they would not capitalise *I*.

I now suspected my students did not see themselves as important enough to capitalise the pronoun *I*. It was as though they thought of themselves as objects belonging to a place like YTC, which is, let's face it, a prison for young men.

Finally, I turned to Bob Marley for help. I brought Marley's "Redemption Song" to play in class. Marc sang the lyrics:

> *Old pirates, yes, they rob I;*
> *Sold I to the merchant ships,*
> *Minutes after they took I*
> *From the bottomless pit...*

"If Jamaican Creole doesn't' use the pronoun *I*, then why is Marley using *I* in this song?" I asked.

They thought for some time and finally, they all put the pieces together: "Because, pirates could physically take him from the ship, but they couldn't rob him of his identity," said Marc. "They couldn't take his sense of self, or his sense of *I*," said Jahmai.

"Slaves could be taken physically from one point to the other, but no one could rob them of their souls," said Shawn and Paul.

Everyone agreed. Marley and I fought the battle of 'I an' I' and I came out on top. In the end, eight young men in YTC began to find a sense of self by capitalising the pronoun *I*.

Dreaming Beyond the Gates of YTC

Passing through one of the grey, metal gates at YTC is a creepy experience. The small, squeaky gate is like a portal to Hades' underworld. The large gate creaks wide open enough to swallow moss-green prison buses or vacuous vans with barking, tracker dogs. Nearly all the students in my CXC English language class would write about those gates that symbolised their new lives.

There is no feeling that matches the somersaults your mind takes when you realise life as you knew it outside has come to an end. For me, time stands still for a few hours every weekend: for the lads inside, it stands still for a three-year sentence – unless they are in remand for a crime like murder. Those young men spend years – three years, five years or more – suspended in time while waiting for a trial date and more years waiting for the trial to finish. Hope becomes a distant dream. Characters in the novels I give them become more vivid than the people they have left behind.

They traded cell phones, computers, Internet and freedom for lives that have come to a screeching halt. To survive, they would have to venture somewhere deep inside of themselves to a place where they couldn't feel the pain they had caused others or the hurt they now felt from their own self-inflicted, wounded lives. Inside YTC, they needed to bury thoughts of home. They needed to follow rules blindly.

This was not the ideal atmosphere for an English teacher who needed students to think and feel and write. Faced with the task of pouring their thoughts and feelings on paper, they would often freeze if they could not readily figure out a connection with the prompt. They had to find a way to face the unexpected. Most of the time they were willing to take chances, but sometimes they just couldn't do it. To fight this fear, I began to toss out short writing prompts in the beginning of class.

One day I said, "You have five minutes to write about the person you would most like to meet in this world. It can be someone who lived in the past or someone who is living today."

Shawn wrote:

> *If I could meet anyone in the world, it would be Jayceon "The Game" Taylor, a multi-platinum-selling rap artiste. With everything he went through, he still found something he loved, succeed in it and become rich. I admire him. His father was a drug addict; his mom was a gang member; his brother died from gang violence. He played basketball well, but he didn't love it so he turned to music. With all his fame and money, he never forgot where he came from. Like me, he had been to jail and he still found a way to make money legally.*

Brian a young man, who came after I made the cut of seven, but left English class for a work programme wrote:

> *I would like to meet Russell Latapy. I love football, and he is one of the best football players in Trinidad and Tobago. I think he can give me some advice.*

Marc wrote:

> *I've heard stories and seen pictures of her, but I have never been blessed with the touch of my great*

grandmother. I only know her as "mama" a name given to her by her grandchildren. Her picture has been hanging over our living room door for ages – she watches us going and coming. I love her. She used to cook the best sweet bread in the whole of Vance River, drink babash and smoke Mt. Dor in our gallery. She would call every single child into our yard and play hide and seek, then let them bathe by our standpipe. Mama Friday, a name I know but have only heard stories about.

My footballer, Kheelon, wrote:

I would like to meet Dwight Yorke because he has plenty experience in football. He could pass it on to me so I could be a better footballer in the future. I could help other young footballers so they can come out successful in life and have a future. I could help my little brother achieve his goals.

Then there was Jahmai's paragraph:

Ever since I knew myself, I lived with my mother and siblings – no memories whatsoever of my father. I have seen him in pictures, but never in person; so for me to meet him – after 19 years of my existence – would be like winning a Nobel Prize. We would talk about things, such as sports, places we have seen, even politics. How happy I would be if I could meet him – if only for a day – before I die. Even if he was sick I would still like to meet with him. After all he is my father.

Most of my students wanted to meet a relative or a famous athlete from Trinidad and Tobago. Their message was clear: When we strip the world of false glitter and gadgets, what matters most are family and the successful people who connect us to life just outside of YTC.

Soon after my students wrote about the people they most wanted to meet, an unexpected visitor came to YTC. Like a miracle conjured up just outside this place for restless souls, the man appeared at those creaking, grey gates. It was Jahmai's dad. When Jahmai told me the news in the next class, I silently hoped that the visit had lived up to all of his dreams. Jahmai never told me if it did.

Christopher "Dudus" Coke in the Classroom

This is bizarre, I thought, as I read my students' essays. I am teaching English to taciturn teenagers dressed in white or brown prison uniforms (with hand-written numbers on them) and my students write with sophisticated punctuation. If colons, semicolons, dashes and commas could be converted to clothes, my students wouldn't be dressed in all white or all brown prison uniforms with three-quarter pants and rubber flip-flops. They'd be dressed in pinstriped suits, silk ties and Gucci shoes.

Take for instance what Marc wrote about *Miguel Street* by V.S. Naipaul:

> It is important to find yourself within the pages of a book: horror, informative, short story – any type of book. Miguel Street *does just that: It draws you in. Even if you are not in a cheerful mood, when you sit or lie down to read* Miguel Street, *you will, I guarantee, cheer up. V.S. Naipaul's* Miguel Street *blows even the most humourless souls on earth away.*

Clearly, somewhere in their past these young men had great teachers who created a solid, academic foundation so that I could complete a two-year CXC English language syllabus in eight months. All I had to do was stick my fingers in some academic holes and plug them up like the proverbial Dutch boy plugging up a leak in a dam.

My main problem was still coming to grips with not using textbooks. Yes, I had been giving them many articles from the Internet that I felt were well written, but I still felt uneasy.

"I can't stand all that irrelevant stuff in the textbooks," I confided in my friend Nadira Akal, a biology teacher.

She said, "Talk to Jenny Woods, an English teacher from Bishop Anstey High School in Port of Spain."

"Trust your instincts," Jenny told me. "You don't have to depend on textbooks. Don't worry about teaching for an exam. Do what you feel you need to do. Do what is best."

I took her advice and finally felt like I was in charge of my own class. I would do things my way. I would no longer worry about the material I used. I would concentrate only on the skills I had to teach. That week I used a series from the *Jamaica Observer* newspaper, "A Gangster's Lament," published on Sunday, September 5, 2010.

My students also read articles about drug lord Christopher "Dudus" Coke. Mark Wilson, who writes geography textbooks for secondary schools, e-mailed me the articles written in Jamaican Creole. That turned out to be an exercise in writing summaries, turning Creole to formal English, and writing analytical essays – all skills to be addressed on the English language syllabus.

The journal would surely show my students that crime didn't pay – at least that's what I thought until I read my students' essays.

Jahmai wrote:

> *Robin Hood to the Kingston, Jamaican ghetto, Tivoli Garden, is what I would have called Christopher "Dudus" Coke. His every move was quite similar to the legendary Robin Hood, who stole from the rich to give to the poor. Dudus' approach was a little different. Instead of robbing the Jamaican government of its currency, he deprived it of its social development*

when he imported and exported drugs and guns to support the needs of the ghetto people along with his own needs.

To law enforcement officers, he was known as the country's most wanted man because of his sinister lifestyle. Fed up of the operations run by Dudus, the government decided that the ghetto hero and his empire had to be destroyed. Putting away Dudus would be no easy task because he was a man who had gained support from the needy. It would cause a rebellion in the ghetto.

All hell broke loose when the law made its move to capture the infamous Christopher "Dudus" Coke. The people of Tivoli Garden started rioting in an attempt to avoid Dudus' capture. Can we be so selfish to blame the people of Tivoli Garden? I wouldn't! Do not get the wrong idea, I am no real supporter of criminal activities, but if I were in their position, I would have done the same. Would you? The people living in places similar to Tivoli face a tremendous amount of trouble finding jobs in Jamaica. Even if they are educated, their residence causes obstacles for them when they try to get jobs.

In the end of this entire chaotic episode, 73 persons were killed while trying to prevent the modern day Robin Hood from being captured. One of those people could have approached the government and brought about some kind of eye opener about the crisis of the ghetto in a more civil way. Instead, Government chose to be aggressive about the matter and went about it the wrong way. I hope the Jamaican government did not just see the whole madness as the people trying to defend wrong, but instead, see it as a cry for help.

My students agreed with Jahmai.

"Dudus helped his neighbourhood," Peter said.

My students didn't see Dudus as a doomed criminal. They felt his life had meaning because he helped poor people that no one cared about. To them, what really mattered is that Dudus didn't turn his back on people like the Jamaican government had done. They didn't see my main point: Dudus's life was doomed because of his life of crime.

I am teaching Martians, I thought, aliens from another planet. Then came a jolting revelation: My students weren't Martians. They lived in another world right here in Trinidad and Tobago.

Ashton Makes a Confession; Shawn Discovers Opera

I never knew what essays I would get from students when I arrived for class. I had encouraged them to keep diaries and write about anything so they handed in assignments and they handed in essays about what was going on in their lives. Clearly, they found it easier to write about their feelings rather than talk about them. Part of that, they would later tell me, came from knowing that I was a writer so they thought writing was very important to me.

They handed in essays about girls they loved and girls they left behind. They handed in essays about their dreams and what their lives would be like someday when they walked out of that YTC gate.

Sometimes they folded letters and secretly handed them to me. Ashton became a prolific letter writer. One day he gave me this:

#9 Book Street
St Ann's Road
Port of Spain,

Dear Mrs Jacob,

I am writing this letter to emphasise my urgent need for some individual attention during the dispensation of your teaching of the English language. It is the opinion of many that a good speaker always makes a good writer. However, although I am always commended and classed as an excellent speaker, writing quickly and appropriately seems to be the hardest thing on earth for me to do.

Most times I do not know where to start. To write the thesis statement of an essay always takes me at least ten minutes. When I finally get started, in no more than three minutes I usually get stuck, and to write a summary at times just feels so impossible.

Please hear my cry, and show me where and how to start. Don't ever feel that I am not interested or making an effort because that would be the furthest thing from the truth. But instead, hear the voice of a willing child, who just doesn't know where and how to start.

Failure is not an option so lead me Mrs Debbie. I am here to follow.

Sincerely yours,
Ashton

This did not come as a surprise to me. I knew Ashton could be the best student in class because of the speeches he wrote for the mentoring programme.

"It's just like writing your speeches," I told him.

I hoped that Ashton could settle down and stop freezing when it came to writing.

In the same class, Shawn handed me an unexpected essay.

Surprises

By Shawn

A couple of weeks ago, I was surprised when Ms Weekes the officer in charge of drama, called my name to attend the second playing of "Misa Cubana". I had no idea what that was, so I enquired.

She explained to me that it was a play based on Christmas. I was surprised that she would even think for a moment that young men would be interested in opera. I was also surprised by how Queen's Hall, St Ann's was decorated for the opera.

As I came out of the bus, I looked across and saw the Hilton Hotel up close and personal. It was the first time that I had ever seen it in real life so it came across a lot larger than it looked on television.

Everything amazed me. I was like a lost puppy in the city. I couldn't even speak. I was just looking around at everyone. They were speaking with accents and wearing expensive jewellery. I felt a little out of place thinking that these people are all rich and I came from jail. I even saw the president, the ex-president and the former Prime Minister Patrick Manning. I saw the Chief Justice and a lot of other people who speak on TV all the time.

I was sitting there just looking at the stage and the people and I realised that everyone there or almost everyone was elderly. I thought to myself I'm going to sleep through this whole thing. They started the show with the anthem, and when I heard the people singing, I thought it was a recording.

Their voices were powerful, so much that they had my utmost attention. Pat Bishop was the director. The best performance for the night was by a lady, I can't remember her name, who sang "Santa Baby". I didn't even sleep a second.

It came to me as a real shocker rather than the usual surprise that I actually liked the play.

Although it was my first time at such a show and I didn't fully understand the theme I promised myself that when I get out "I will visit another opera."

Before that night I was never interested in that type of music. I listen to all genres of music or most of them, but I am now interested in opera. The boys say it's "nerdy", but I don't care.

By Christmas, I sat in Queen's Hall with Shawn and my other students and six guards on an approved YTC outing to see the Marionettes' Christmas concert.

There I was, a reclusive English teacher sitting in a row of singing guards gazing over 15 astonished YTC inmates.

The Marionettes and their conductor Gretta Taylor conjured up a magical afternoon for Shawn, who loves opera, and the rest of my students who had never experienced a performance like that Christmas offering.

I thought about how much we had gone through as a class in three short months. Sometimes it seemed like we wouldn't make it to the end of the year, but we did, and we all learned so much about ourselves.

My students squirmed at the first high note a soprano hit. A tenor voice forced them to flash nervous smiles. It's amazing how uncomfortable young people can be with soft melodies and meaningful lyrics. This, I thought, is a far cry from the hate-filled, angry rap music that defines their lives. Uncomfortable with the unknown, they whispered, fidgeted and drifted in and out of a dreamy sleep.

In their insecurity with new experiences, my group would later say that it was strange music, but for one hour my young men experienced the true holiday spirit. They had never heard anyone sing "Bridge Over Troubled Water", the Simon and Garfunkel hit that I loved when I was younger than them. Many of the songs my generation takes for granted have never been part of their lives.

When I was growing up, we heard pop, jazz, rock, gospel, and country – a rich blend of music on the radio. We listened to sad songs and happy songs; love songs and survival songs. We experienced every emotion through our music, and this helped us to grow as individuals. Perhaps therein lies the problem with young people today: they just don't hear and see and feel all the emotions we experienced in our music.

There's no feeling in the world like hearing a choir sing the "Hallelujah Chorus" from Handel's *Messiah*. This is the memory that I carried away from the Marionettes' concert; this, and the memory of many young people from all the homes for lost or physically or mentally challenged children who could feel the Gift of Peace if only for one afternoon in that special Christmas show.

Every year, the Marionettes think about these forgotten children and young people of Trinidad and Tobago. They don't have to devote a performance to children who can't afford to buy tickets, but they do. That is what you call true Christmas spirit.

Resolutions

I once felt that a list of New Year's resolutions was mandatory for marching into a new year. I thought if we all wrote lists, we'd have plans that would magically materialise. Now, I realise that the wisdom with which we greet a new year comes from all the painful and difficult lessons we have learned from the year that we leave behind.

Knowing this, I could face the New Year with a sigh of relief. By the end of the year, I had grown a little braver and a little more confident. There were still many things I couldn't face, like how much I wanted to know about my students. As they began to open up more and write more about their lives, I wondered: should I really know this?

Every Saturday night when I left my CXC English language class and walked across the grounds of YTC, my heart sank as I heard my students standing behind the metal gates and calling into the darkness, "Bye Miss. Be careful on the road."

One by one the sadness in their voices would ring through the night like heavy, mournful church bells. I learned to answer lads, who were not in my class, when they said, "Good night, good afternoon, hello and goodbye" without looking at them. I'd look just beyond them. If I don't see the pain or hurt or sadness or desperation in their faces, I reasoned, I wouldn't have to feel guilty that I couldn't help them.

It's hard to realise there's only so much you can do. It's difficult to see so many boys who need something or someone: a new t-shirt, a visit from a relative, love, an apple, a smile.

Even in my own class, I didn't know how things would turn out. I had made up my mind from the beginning if I could save just one student, my time in YTC be worthwhile. If I could just keep at least one from coming back outside and doing something worse, it would be an accomplishment.

Outside YTC, the lights always seemed brighter and the world seemed to be pulsing like a heartbeat. Week after week, I managed to survive the madness of driving down the highway. I could breathe a sigh of relief when I reached Cipriani Boulevard in Port of Spain where a bevy of women in their spiked heels and an army of liming men in their Nike shoes traipsed towards the direction of music blasting from some night spot. As I watched all those laughing people, I imagined my students settling down in the dim YTC light to read *I Beat the Odds* by Michael Oher or *Uncommon* by Tony Dungy before they decided to write a letter to me. Nearly every class at least one student – usually Jahmai, Shawn or Ashton – slipped me a letter of thanks or encouragement. I kept them to read when I got home.

I would sit in my living room with my dogs, Rambo and Duchess, at my feet as I read my letters and cried. Their essays always featured something they wanted to share about their lives or schoolwork. Their letters were always about me; some weakness they had picked up. They had made me their cause. They wanted to toughen me up.

No matter how hard I tried to be a confident teacher, I feared the unknown: a CXC exam I had never taught for. I was afraid of failing. I had made a wild promise to do a two-year syllabus in eight months and since then I had learned I had so much more to do than teaching. Most of the time it felt like 20 per cent of my job was teaching academic "stuff". I still struggled to develop trust.

No teaching can take place without trust, and that was a slippery slope that both my students and I had to climb. My students were very short on trust in general, and I suspected it was even more difficult for them to trust me because I was – let's face it – a bit strange. I was a foreign, white woman with strange notions of teaching.

I never gave grades, and my students never asked for grades. I had a lower tolerance for boring material than they had. I liked tight, edgy writing with a slam dunk beginning – not that horrible, loose idea of an "introduction" that they knew from school. I preached that in order to do well on this exam they would have to read, read, read. Reading, I argued, was more important than any teaching I could do.

"There's nothing in the syllabus that says you have to read novels. The syllabus suggests that you read, but I'm telling you that reading is your lifeline. You have to read so you can develop the speed and concentration you need to get through this English exam. You have to read to develop the analytical skills you need to do well. Besides, I am not a teacher who is going to hand out vocabulary lists. You have to develop your vocabulary through your reading. Trust me."

"Trust me," I kept saying, but I didn't trust myself. All I knew was that I couldn't just teach for a test. I had to teach my students how to think and feel and use language so that they could navigate their way through real-life challenges rather than just react out of anger.

On the road to trust, I knew I had to break the formality between us. I needed to know more about my students outside of class so that I could find reading and writing exercises that would interest them. I began bringing food: cheese paste sandwiches and chocolate cakes; a macaroni and tuna fish pie because their last meal for the day was at 3:30 p.m.

The more we talked, the more we trusted each other. Communication will do that. The more we trusted each other, the more I cried when I reached home every Saturday night. The closer I got to them, the more frightened I got of letting them down.

Looking back, I realise my students gradually gave me their trust so that I could gain confidence as their teacher. I know how much they sensed my fears. Although I had a long way to go in those early stages, I headed into the new year with a growing feeling of confidence I had never had my whole life because my students taught me to trust myself. They refused to give up on me.

There I was, this strange teacher, a social recluse who did nothing but go to work, come home, curl up on the couch with a good book and read, hang out with my two pitbulls, Duchess and Rambo, and write. I was no master of communication and I wouldn't register on a scale of social skills, but I had to figure out the skills they would need to fit into society someday.

I knew, deep down, that these boys deserved a lot better than me, but I was all they had for a CXC English language teacher.

I had learned a lot. I had learned not to run away from fear or discomfort. Stick it out, I told myself, and I was doing just that: taking one day at a time.

Off the Wall

It didn't take long for me to predict the mood of every single class. A couple of months after we settled in, I realised that everything had changed. My students were no longer unquestionably compliant. At first I hadn't noticed, and when I did, I tried to put it out of my mind. Finally I recognised the pattern. One week everyone – with the exception of Ashton – would be cold and distant. They'd cram themselves together like sardines in a tin, and they'd sit as close to the door as they could. They wouldn't misbehave. They'd zone out. They wouldn't watch me. They'd fold their arms or lean forward in their chairs and stare down at their books. Some would report to the guard that they felt sick and not come to class.

Ashton, on the other hand, would give me the third degree about some current events: what did I think the teenage girls in the newspaper stories were doing when they ran away from home?

"I don't know?" I'd say.

"Yes, you do, Miss. They're looking for man." I felt shocked, sometimes, how judgmental and self-righteous they could be about others. They really came off as being very conservative – at least when it came to other people's behaviour.

Sometimes Ashton would give a report on the times my name came up in the news or when a story I wrote had been mentioned on the radio. Ashton, always his usual talkative self, paused only to ask for advice on the book he was writing about his experiences. He still kept confessing he couldn't write essays. No matter what I tried, Ashton would freeze and produce no more than a few sentences for every in-class writing assignment. The agony registered on his face.

Ashton's unwavering, upbeat personality and that way he had of making a totally disorganised person like me feel on top of everything just because he sat in the same room, proved to be a crutch for me. I would lean on Ashton a lot and marvel at his ability to remove himself emotionally from the darkness that sometimes loomed over class.

Even on the worst days, the lads would muster enough politeness to allow me to drag answers out of them, but they sounded and looked like zombies. They didn't want to eat the cheese paste sandwiches or cake I brought. They moped and whined about everything: the food in prison (they claimed you could kill someone if you pelted your bread at him). The place was dirty: too many flies. They had a litany of woes.

I shrugged and said, "Well, you didn't exactly check yourselves into the Hilton Hotel."

The next week, without fail, they'd be effervescent – totally bubbling over with joy. They couldn't sit close enough to me. They'd rush to arrange the room, and scoop all the books from my hands. They greeted me with "Hey, Miss" like I had been a lost relative or friend. They eagerly participated in class. Every right answer registered like they had hit the jackpot. Impulsivity popped up in their answers at times, but they were learning to use a process to think through a question.

No description could capture the joy on their faces when I praised them for giving a right answer. As they grew creatively, they garnered their praise with beaming smiles, a big change from the days when they wouldn't own up to an answer because they thought they would be criticised for it, like when Olton took minutes to own up to his answer about wanting to be a turtle on that first day of class.

Good days felt spectacular – a genuine feeling of accomplishment. Marc became the best student in grammar exercises, and Jahmai quickly proved to be his rival. Never to disappear into the crowd, Shawn strived to top the grammar exercises.

Marc got those stupid exercises where you have to change and rearrange part of the sentence. He delivered those answers at a blistering pace. I find those exercises so difficult and frustrating because you have to change parts of the sentence that often aren't underlined. They literally give me a headache. While I tried to figure out the answer, Marc blurted it out and the whole class erupted in "ohhhhhhh."

They got excited when I said things like "You have to learn the grammar rules so that you will know how to break them."

Breaking any type of rules seemed enticing.

"People say you can't start a sentence with a conjunction like 'and', but what if you want to make a point like you want to show boredom or tediousness like Hemingway did in *A Farewell to Arms* when he strings together pages of sentences with 'and' in almost every sentence to show the tediousness of a war that dragged on and on. What if you want something to stand out?

"What if you want to create a mood or tone?

"If you don't know the rules, and you break them you look like you don't know what you're doing, and you always want to look like you know what you're doing."

We discussed how people use language to manipulate.

They said, "Ads do that, Miss, and the Government."

I asked them, "Who do you think is the best person I have ever met in terms of being able to manipulate language?"

"A government minister?" they guessed.

"No."

"A preacher?"

"Well, someone in religion," I said, and without hesitation they guessed Yasin Abu Bakr, the Muslim Imam responsible for the 1990 coup attempt in Trinidad and Tobago.

"And don't forget this," I said, "When given the choice,

always write what you know about: write about your own experiences. We write best about the things we know, but don't scare people to death," I said, and they laughed.

On a good day I could get them to think enthusiastically about anything I threw out to challenge them. One day I said, "Do you know what the best form of revenge is?"

Silence…Then they erupted in a sea of echoes. "Tell us, Miss. Tell us. Tell us…."

"Happiness," I said.

They look puzzled.

"People like to see you angry or sad because it gives them a sense of power to destabilise you, but what many people really can't take is genuine happiness. They can't stand to see someone happy," I said.

And so I rode that roller coast up and down through all those gut wrenching dips and climbs, anxiously anticipating the worst Saturdays and Sundays and joyfully celebrating the coming week when I knew they would rise to the occasion. But it was tough, and it wore me down. Finally, I confided in Ms McDonald.

"Did you talk to them about it?" she asked.

"No, I'm afraid I'll disturb some kind of rhythm in them that they need to go forward. I'll talk to them after the exam," I said.

"It's best to talk to them now," she said. "Whenever something happens, talk to them right away."

"That's what I'd normally do, but with them…."

"Stop being afraid of them," she said.

"I'm not afraid; I just don't want to upset them."

"They're already upset about so many things, and yes, you're afraid: you're afraid you'll upset them. Don't be afraid. Treat them like you'd treat any boys."

The next time my students became sullen, I confronted them. "You know you can't have any relationship with anyone if you smother them one minute and shove them away the next," I said. "You can't have girlfriends if you do that – at least not good ones. No girl who is worth anything will put up with that behaviour. If something is bothering you, you have to deal with it appropriately. That means you talk about it."

Case closed. From then on, they worked through the tough and rough times. They learned to put words to feelings: mad, sad and glad, but of course they would never admit to feeling scared.

For the Love of Reading

When I got to YTC, I parked my car and walked, as usual, over to the gate to ask the guard if someone could help me with the books I had brought for class. As I asked the guard, two boys came up with a cooler that they had been instructed to place outside of the gate. One of the boys told the other one, "That is my English teacher."

"That's your English teacher," he said.

"Yes, CXC English."

"Really?" he asked.

Kheelon asked the guard, "Can I help her? She's my teacher."

The guard said yes.

The two boys walked behind me and my student said, "You know how long it's been since I walked the street?"

When we got to the car, Kheelon saw the book *Cracker! The Best Dog in Viet Nam* by Cynthia Kadohata and asked if he could have it because he's been reading it. I had given it to one of the students last week. Kheelon told me about the boy having to give up the dog because he lived in an apartment. He said, "It's a really good book. I'd like to have one of my own."

While we waited for other students to come to class, Kheelon told me that he had not done any subjects for CXC. "I told my mother I wanted to do a trade and I was studying to be an electrician."

Kheelon was finishing his studies to be an electrician inside YTC.

Practice for a drama production meant I was missing a few students including Friday. I brought *Robinson Crusoe* by

Daniel Defoe for Friday to read. You can't have a last name of Friday and not read Robinson Crusoe.

I wanted to get the boys used to settling to write very quickly. They were so concerned about the rules for everything, but they had a tendency to procrastinate when it came to writing in class. They spent so much time trying to establish the boundaries and the rules for a writing assignment. I suspected it was just fear to take the plunge but I worried they would sit in an exam and never get started, never take the opportunity to show how much they had learned or how far they had come in their writing. I asked them to write an essay about what makes them Trinidadian or West Indian. They could choose. No one chose West Indian. Many couldn't write anything. One doodled across the page, made several attempts to try and scratched everything off.

I told them to just write without thinking if they couldn't think of anything. Just let ideas flow. They wrote about Trinidad for the most part rather than themselves. They said they like to party and they like Carnival and Soca music.

"Soca makes us a great country and oil, the Pitch Lake."

They all sounded like advertisements. They didn't really address what made them Trinidadians.

That day, after class, I gave them some sandwiches I had made. My students picked up the plastic bread bag after they doled out the sandwiches and looked at the price of bread.

"This is how much bread is now?" they gasped. "When I was out there…." They all began to measure their time inside YTC with the cost of bread when they lived outside.

I had bought several copies of *Upstate* by Kalisha Buckhanon. One of the boys had asked me for it. He had seen a review I had written in the newspaper. I had four copies. I asked who else wanted to read the book. No one volunteered.

I said, "This is the only book I ever got in trouble for having in the library."

Everybody's hand shot up for a copy of the book. When I told them it was about a boy in prison trying to maintain relationships with people outside, they leaped from their seats, clenched their mouths shut and waved their hands frantically.

"All of you should have a copy of *Upstate*," I said.

As time went on, their taste in books would grow in an interesting way. At first they wanted action-packed, plot-driven books – "lots of excitement" they said, "and some romance too."

Then they wanted books about boys in prison. This emerged after they read *Upstate.*

"That's just how it is in here," they said of *Upstate*. "Your girl leaves you – dumps you for someone else, and it have boys in here too, just like in the book, who take a rap for a younger brother. You know, Miss, there are innocent people in here too."

I did not doubt that. Then they wanted stories with some meaning like *Of Mice and Men* by John Steinbeck. They enjoyed books like *To Kill a Mockingbird* by Harper Lee. Olton started an avalanche of interest in "books to make you a better person".

Olton, a star rugby player for YTC and the Trinidad and Tobago National Under-19 national team, dreamed of being an American NFL football player. He wanted to read *The Blind Side* by Michael Lewis because he had seen the movie about Michael Oher, the African American boy taken in by the Tuohys, a rich, white family. Oher would eventually become a professional football player for the Baltimore Ravens.

Then, Olton wanted to read *In a Heartbeat: Sharing the Power of Cheerful Giving* by Leigh Anne Tuohy, Sean Tuohy and Sally Jenkins.

Of course he then wanted to read *I Beat the Odds*, Michael Oher's book about how he survived the poverty, drugs and crime in his neighbourhood.

Eventually everyone gravitated toward Coach Tony Dungy's book *Uncommon*, a practical guide about being an individual who rises above the crowd. This became one of the most popular reads, replaced eventually by *Like Water for Elephants* by Sara Gruen. They enjoyed the romance and the story of a young man who runs away to join the circus. Who wouldn't like to run away and join the circus?

The Ship is Sinking

I tried to start every class with a writing exercise so that my students could get used to timed writings. I also wanted them to practise interpreting abstract or symbolic things. One day I gave my students this prompt:

"The ship was sinking. I was asked to take the most important item in my life. The next thing I knew, I woke up on a deserted island."

That was trouble. Rather than deal with the assignment, someone wrote it was all a dream. One boy said he took a torch light. One boy took a picture of his mother. The rest took a cell phone or a knife.

They had a difficult time conceptualising anything symbolic. They could relate to feelings – if they could identify with the feelings personally, but empathy proved to be a challenge for them.

It took them forever to settle and write. They constantly worried about the rules. They had this in common with almost all student writers: They started back too far when they wrote. They wrote about how they got on the island when they were supposed to be on the island already.

Memories
By Marc Friday

The wind blew fiercely. She screamed and cried, bending the tall palm trees in her rage. Any minute I could expect rain, but I was safe from that – I was in a cave infested with ants and fruit bats. I continued to walk deeper into the darkness, my hand in my pocket and my faith with my God.

On October 27th, 1932 our ship – Beauty's Beast – got shipwrecked on an island somewhere in the Caribbean. It was a heart-stopping event, literally for my whole crew, figuratively for me. I could barely swim and without my glasses I was blind as a bat, but I held on, hoping one day to see her again: Muriel Lawrence from Glasgow, England.

Captain told me to take only one item with me from the ship. I took the only thing that touched my heart since the Civil War: a ribbon used to tie Muriel's hair. It still had the rosy scent that made my goose bumps rise.

The next thing I knew, I was on a deserted island with nothing but the clothes on my back and the ribbon. Muriel helped me survive two months of eating fruits and raw fish from in the river. The memory of roses, her smile, her blue-ocean eyes and blond, silky hair; the memory of love and joy and her cute dimples that appeared when she smiled her Greek goddess smile were all I had.

Alone

By Shawn

The sound of the wave hitting rocks woke me. I looked around and for a moment I seemed to have amnesia.

"Where am I?" I was asking out loud, but it seemed like I was the only one on the island. Then it all began coming back to me: I was on a cruise ship. It was sinking fast. I managed to acquire a Ziploc bag and I thought to myself what should I take with me in case I was to survive. My cell phone seemed like it was the most important thing to me.

I quickly began feeling my jacket pocket for the Ziploc bag. It was still a little wet on the outside, but the Blackberry Curve was perfectly dry. I turned on the phone and immediately looked at the service bars. It didn't have any. For a while I raised it in the air trying to get service, but then I realised that there weren't any service towers around so I took it off.

I began feeling hungry. This wasn't a problem because of my background. I was just a lucky lifeguard who lived on the beaches of Mayaro. That was the south-eastern coast of Trinidad to be exact. I had won a cruise ship ticket while surfing for being the 100th visitor. Back home I fished a lot, and I hunted a lot. I spent a lot of time on the beach due to my occupation (lifeguard).

I began feeling hungry, but I was too weak to fend for myself. I heard a chopper in the distance and with one last attempt at being rescued from the deserted island tried to wave to the helicopter. I got no response. Who was I kidding? The helicopter could be 100 miles away.

It was then I made up my mind to die. I saw the chopper passing again and I didn't even bother to try. I had nothing: I was hungry and cold and night was falling.

I closed my eyes on the verge of death and I began thinking "What have I done with my life?"

The first thing I ever won in my whole life was the last. I thought back to my job and recalled all the times I heard all the voices on the radio "over and out" and "roger that". It was then I remembered the Blackberry had walkie talkie mode. I drained my last ounce of energy, climbed a tree and turned on the phone again.

When I heard the helicopter pilot come over, a burst of relief hit me.

So the phone, which I saw as the most important item to me at the time I left the ship, saved my life. And knowing the channels helped me even more.

How Much Do I Want to Know?

*I had fallen asleep on the couch watching "The Closer".
Somewhere, in a distant dream, I heard someone calling,
"Good night, good night." One of my son Jairzinho's friends
was at the gate.   "I'm Max," he said.*

I checked the time: 1:00 a.m. Sunday morning.

"I work at Angelo's. I just got off work. We had a busy night. The President stopped by," said Max, "and everything had to be up to mark."

Nodding, I studied the young man talking excitedly about his Saturday night, and I thought: he's doing a job he loves. He's free to finish work, walk out the door and lime with some friends. I thought of my boys inside YTC. They would not have the opportunity to be carefree teenagers. They couldn't even play tough any more. Now, they were locked away in a dirty prison battling nothing more than the flies that have become so aggressive in there they dive at your face like some fighter jet aiming for its target.

As Max talked more and more about himself, his job and his fantastic night, it suddenly occurred to me that a teacher generally wants to know everything she can about her students. Without asking, she has some idea of their background and interests. She meets their parents and works with parents on a course of action.

This was not my case. I knew very little about my students, and I had never met their parents. Would it help me to know more about their backgrounds or would it make everything harder? Would I be frightened, sad or just turned off? All I really knew is that my students were put in YTC by the court.

I know there are many people who believe that we should take anyone who has committed a crime – even teenagers – toss them in prison, lock the gate and throw the key away.

But the problem is most of these lads will be out on the street some day. Isn't it better to try to do something with them? If they are educated, I argued with myself, they'll be in a better position to think for themselves. They'll have more opportunities.

It wasn't until much later that I would learn from a prison social worker that many of the boys inside YTC – including some of mine – came from places that qualify for something even below poverty: utter squalour.

"Even when they get out," the social worker told me, "their lives are always in danger. The pressure on them is unbelievable. They have to have real willpower to walk away from their past. Those gangs out there won't leave them alone."

For me, it had always been sad to think about a class at my school, the International School of Port of Spain, ending, but I felt happy knowing my students were going out in the world most likely to go to university. They would be well taken care of by their families. I was afraid of what would happen to these teenagers.

I tried not to think about what they had done to be placed in YTC. The worst it could be was violent, armed robbery, I thought. I couldn't fathom anything worse than that.

The Monday after Max showed up at my gate, I called Mr Stewart, about taking my students on an outing.

"I don't think you have any students in your class who are in remand for murder," he said. "Let me check the list. Oh you do have a couple."

That news made me turn cold. I gasped.

Mr Stewart realised I had never been told about the boys in remand for capital murder charges. I was dumb enough at that time not to figure out that they were the boys who still wore civilian clothes while boys convicted, boys with three-year sentences wore the brown or white uniforms of YTC.

"No, no, don't feel like that," Mr Stewart said. "All of these boys are here because society believes they can be rehabilitated. Many of those murder cases are abuse cases or school fights."

I saw things now in a whole new light. I had done reasonably well, I thought, pushing aside my feelings about those who were in for robbery even though I knew so many people who had been robbed.

Once, I had a car stolen. When my children, Ijanaya and Jairzinho, were only three and two, someone had broken into my home at night when I was in the house. I grabbed a knife, held Jairzinho in my arms and screamed my head off until the thief took everything he wanted in my house.

I know I fared better than many people who had been robbed. No one touched me or hurt me – at least not in a way you could see.

I had installed a wrought-iron gate between my living room and the rest of the house and made my living room a no-man's-land for over a decade. I didn't get a good night's sleep for ten years. Every time a dog barked, I woke up. It wasn't until I decided to keep Duchess the pitbull for her owner, Dane Quesnel, who left Trinidad and Tobago to work in Anguilla, that I finally slept through an entire night.

Instead of looking back on how they had hurt people, I kept imagining the person I might help save in the future if I could help these teenagers to learn how to think and feel and empathise on a whole new level so they wouldn't come out to do something worse – like murder.

Now I had to figure out how to deal with knowing there were boys who had already committed murder. Mr Stewart was talking to me, and I didn't know how much I had missed. When I finally tuned in once again, he was saying, "All these boys need is love. That is the only thing that is wrong with them. Love, they need someone to love them."

Somehow, that calmed me down. After much thought, I came to the conclusion that even the lads who were in for murder would most likely have the charges reduced to manslaughter. They would be out some day. It was better to do something with them than nothing so when I returned to class, I knew exactly what to say when Ashton hit me one day with "Miss, I have to ask you a question. How does it feel to be teaching boys and young men who have done crimes – and some of them heinous crimes? Tell me the truth, Miss, and don't sugar-coat it."

Without hesitation, I said, "I can't think about where you came from or where you are now. I can only think about where you are going. I can only think about your future."

"That's a good answer, Miss," Ashton said.

It was the only answer that made any sense to me.

I See Myself

In light of what I had learned, I thought it might be a good exercise for my class to think more about themselves, and so I gave an assignment: Write an essay entitled "I See Myself…."

Most of my students welcomed the opportunity to write about themselves. They beamed big smiles and looked like a huge load had been taken off their shoulders. There was always this feeling that they wanted to write about how they felt, but they were, no doubt, afraid of how much they could reveal without pushing me away.

"They have abandonment issues," Ms McDonald had told me once, "and plenty of them don't know how to act. Some have had to fight so hard to survive, they got to a stage where all they could do is react to what was being thrown at them every minute. These aren't boys who act: these are boys who react to what's around them."

They wrote moving essays. Shawn outlined his argument and then wrote a brutally honest, personal essay.

I See Myself
Shawn

Outline:

1. *Theme – smart*

2. *I see myself as a smart person*

3. *Why? I always take time to think through everything.*

4. I see myself as a smart person who always knows the right thing but chooses the wrong things.

5. I use my sense to do the wrong things

I see myself as a smart person because believe it or not, I am really smart; I use my mind to think through the wrong things and the right things to outsmart people. I never run into anything without firstly analysing the whole situation. In my whole life, I see myself as very smart, and I always know the right things even when I am doing wrong.

In the past, I have used my intelligence to develop ideas to do the wrong things such as rob people or to acquire illegal things. I even sat and thought out whole crime scenes.

I am trying to be honest because these are things that have really happened to me in real. Some of my seemingly genius ideas worked. Some worked for a little while and others never prevailed so for sure that wasn't what I was supposed to use my smartness for. I still get temptations to plot up ideas – even in here – but resist those thoughts.

In the past I have used my mind to outsmart people. I sold them things my whole life for prices that were way over priced. I always came up with lies to the questions people had and kept them thinking that I was a good boy when really I wasn't bad either but just thought I could outsmart the whole world.

I also used my intelligence for the right things most of the time. I seemed to be the smartest in most of my classes in school: plumbing, computer classes, football. I was the captain of my football team because I was able to look at the training, see what everyone had to do and direct them on the field so smartness carried me my whole life.

Being so smart made me versatile. I was able to look at any situation, think about it and adapt to the situation. My whole life I have been smart, so it is nothing new, but just making wrong decisions landed me in YTC. I always thought I could outsmart everyone; I could outsmart the world.

Dear Shawn,

You are much too intelligent to be in so much trouble. You can put your mind to good use. That will happen only when you realise what a true sense of power is. Yes, it's possible to fool people, but that's not real power. Real power – and independence – will come when you can expose who you really are under the masks you wear. That goes for everyone. You are a very interesting and smart person. I see that every time you write and every time you talk.

Sincerely,
Miss

Kheelon Mitchell

I see myself as an athlete because of the different sports I can play such as football, track and field, swimming and basketball. I have been involved in sports for about ten years. My mother encouraged me to keep playing sports and not give up because she realised that was the only thing I was comfortable doing. And it helped me to control my anger and have discipline. It helped me to deal with other people on the same team with me and not put them down.

I first started swimming with our school. I wanted to go to a swim meet. Then the coach told me that we were having a swim meet in the Marvin Lee Stadium. I told her that I was going to come, but only swim in two races I won't take part in all. She told me that she would sign me up for the two races I wanted to

91

do. The first medal I got for swimming was gold for coming first in freestyle. I was the only one to win a medal that day.

Once, I was liming on the wall by me and this coach come and told me that he heard I could goal keep and I told him yes. He told me that he was bringing out a football team and he wanted me to come and train with his team. I asked him when he was training and he told me tomorrow and I told him ok. The next day, I went out and trained with the team. The boys were bigger than me. But I did well.

I got trophies and medals in football, and that gave me more encouragement to keep playing. I used to play with United Petrotrin. That was the first time I played pro league and I was the goalkeeper for the team. Then I went to play with Joe Public and that experience was very good for a young footballer like myself. I was very happy to play out of my home town. There was a screening for the national Under-Seventeen team and that was very hard for me because of where I was from. That coach had his favourites, and I was not one of them so I got cut off of the team. Right now this Under-Twenty team is good so I have a better chance of making this team.

I also liked basketball because it is a very active game. One day my friends told me that it have a basketball league opening and then wanted to know if I am interested. I was interested in playing and I told them yes, I was. I was a little frightened because I didn't understand the game. I played until I understood the game. I shot a lot of points in the rest of the games. The coach started to play me in the starting five every game.

I think all these sports helped me to build my character and my belief in what I can do. I can do anything I want to do in…. (Ends here)

Dear Kheelon,

I'm curious to know what the missing word is in the end of your essay. Why didn't you put that word in? I was very impressed with the structure of your essay, and the support you gave for readers to see why you think of yourself as an athlete. I admire your bravery when it comes to writing. You never write less than a two-page essay even though you always find formal English a challenge, you always try. That attitude will take you a long way. Keep writing.

Sincerely,
Miss

P.S. Notice how you can write in formal English, but you slip back into Creole (It have) near the end of the essay?

About Me!

By Jahmai

Today a most resentful remark was made upon my life "You like Jail," by my ever graceful superintendent. If it was not only thought about today, then by seeing me exercise in the EXERCISE YARD was the final straw that broke the camel's back, that made him come up with this powerful remark.

Since this exercise yard does not contain any weight lifting machines, inmates use full buckets of water to form weights. I do not quite understand how he assembled the idea that lifting weights in prison means that someone likes jail. Is it not true that people lift weights for building muscles? Is it not also true that people outside of prison lift weights?

Jahmai is my name. Jahmai means "May the Lord protect." I am full of emotions, not only of hate and anger, as some people seem to believe. Sometimes I switch from one emotion to the other as fast as the snap of a finger. It is one of my bitter faults that I am trying to put a leash on and control. At present my occupational dream is to become a psychologist. I am full of hope that I will accomplish my goal. Anything I am challenged with, I try to overcome with fine style and perfection.

I appreciate tasks that can be challenging like the books I am reading at present (please laugh. No disrespect intended). Also to leave out of this essay, about myself, that I love my family, especially my mother, Susan Grace Donaldson, will totally be inconsiderate of me. I have made personal defeating choices that were in absolute defiance of her teachings and I am truly sorry. I am extremely thankful to all the people that try to help me become a real man of understanding and responsibility.

Sometimes I may rebel at the helpful pushes of good-willed people but not because of ignorance, but because of my bitter faults, the mood swings that seem to engulf my life. I know my heart, it is not dark, I am not evil, I do not like jail, but I am thankful for the second chance that jail has given me to get an education.

These are my ambitions, goals, setbacks and faults at present. I am trying to achieve my positive dreams and extinguish all faults and setbacks in a way that others may find easy to follow. I must say that we are all human beings so I allow whoever is without sin to condemn me. I am willing to accept correction.

Dear Jahmai,

I always love your style, and your willingness to face your feelings. I don't think that you are evil either. You are an intelligent young man with your whole life ahead of you, and it's going to be great. I believe in you.

Sincerely
Miss

About Me, Peter

I am a funny, loving, dedicated, responsible person, but most of all I am loyal. I can also be a dread person because I have an anger problem. Sports, money and women are the things I love in life including family and friends. I don't deal with religion, but I believe there is a true and living God.

I was born in Trinidad, and lived in another Caribbean country until I came back to Trinidad to live when I was about 11. By the time I was eight, I was a chronic gambler: card games, dice – any game. As a youth growing up, I was exposed to a life of crime; my life took a big turn: I started to cheat people, rob, lie…. I rebelled against order, and I was all over the place.

I grew up in a dog-eat-dog place, never really getting the support from my family to be something good in life. Most of my life I lived without my mother. She couldn't be with me. She was travelling around to different countries selling clothes. In Trinidad, I stayed with an aunt. I got fed three meals a day and then it was like you can do whatever you want so I lashed out at people. My relatives didn't really care about my education and my bahaviour. I didn't mention my father in the above because although he is alive, in my life he is dead. Experiencing these problems in my life helped build up an anger inside me, which had me doing all kinds of evil things. Although I figure my family wasn't being loyal to me and my upbringing, I still love them, and I will always be loyal to them.

I lived in two different towns. I was back and forth and I was caught in the crossfire between two rival gangs. I knew both gangs: I was in the middle of both gangs. Gang leaders look for someone like me with a venomous anger. Anger got me in trouble.

In my 18 years of life I have been in a fair amount of relationships with women. Plenty of them didn't like me for me, but for what I have and who I am in my neighbourhood. Although I know plenty women are a trap, I don't think all of them are the same so I would always be loyal to them and treat them the way they are supposed to be treated.

I always find the time to take part in sports because I love them. I knew I had talent in football and cricket. My favourite sports are cricket and football; my favourite cricket and football teams are West Indies and Arsenal. I am loyal to both teams although they haven't won anything for a while now.

At this present moment in my life, I am in a situation only God could take me out of successfully. While I am hoping for God to grant me some favour, I am trying to gain a proper education and to be something good in life. I also want to help youths and show them the right way how to go about life. I want to be there for them when they need somebody to love them and to guide them. I want them to know they have a loyal friend, I Peter.

Dear Peter,

You are always so quiet in class so I was quite surprised to get this essay about you.

Sincerely,
Miss

Revelation Time

As I read Kheelon's essay about how sports had defined his life, it hit me: My students' papers had been filled with corrections that were basically the same issues repeated over and over. My students weren't really making serious grammatical errors. They were using Trinidad Creole. Some problems were embedded in their Creole like using will **for** would**.**

On the other hand, they mastered structure quickly. Their punctuation was amazing. Most of my students had not been exposed to formal English so they were willing to make corrections, and prepare the essays how I wanted them.   Kheelon would re-write an essay seven times to get it into its final shape, as he did with the essay about how sports defined his life.

I don't know why this all hit me like some epiphany. My students always spoke in Creole, and they always wrote in Creole, it just didn't register with me. I had come to accept that in secondary school, boys generally speak in Creole while girls usually speak in formal English. Perhaps I didn't put two and two together because no one – including me – expects young men who are in an institution – namely the prison system – to be functioning at the level, academically speaking, that my students were performing at.

We think of the stereotypic image of "prisoners" having severe learning issues or functioning, academically speaking, at a primary school level. We don't expect to see bright young men like my students who could articulate sophisticated ideas.

The good news was that my students could write well – in Creole. That meant they'd be able to transfer those skills to formal English as long as they were treated as second language speakers.

This was not a wild idea that I pulled out of the air. Linguists from the University of the West Indies, St Augustine, have been talking or writing about this situation in Trinidad and Tobago for years.

When I had attended the Trinidad and Tobago's Ministry of Education's National Forum on Literacy in Primary Education, some interesting facts emerged.

Professor Ian Robertson, a linguist who worked in education at the university level before he retired, said studies had determined that English (formal English) is the second language for 85 per cent of the Trinidad and Tobago population. Here was the breakdown of first languages in Trinidad:

Hindi – 10%
Spanish – 3%
Yoruba – 1%
Arabic – 3%
Sign language – 3%
Creole – 85% (There is some overlap here because some
        students speak a Creole that includes Hindi.)

Dr Robertson said studies showed that most Trinidadian students should be treated as ESOL (English Speakers of Other Languages) students. He talked about some specific studies of the Syrian student population that linked poor academic performance to second language issues which no one ever picked up because they assumed that English was their first language when Arabic really was.

Of course realising all of this after I had read Kheelon's essay propelled me into a state of panic once again. I'm not trained as an ESOL teacher, and my students needed an ESOL teacher. I tried to explain this to my students.

"You're not really making mistakes when you write, I told them. "You're writing in another language. Creole. That's your first language."

At first Ashton, Kheelon, Marc, Jahmai, Peter, Vaughn, Olton and Shawn looked puzzled.

"Are you sure, Miss?" they asked.

"Yes, and you have very good Creole grammar," I said.

"Now, you just have to learn what the equivalent is in formal English. That's a whole new subject: like taking Spanish or French in school. It's a whole new discipline."

When they finally began to buy into what I was saying, they beamed proud smiles. There's nothing in the world like the smile on a student's face when he realises he's not making mistakes because usually they equate mistakes with being dumb.

What I relish about being a teacher is that there is always someone to turn to when you're in trouble. Other teachers become invaluable resources, and so it was I turned to Eniko Bihari, an ESOL teacher in my school. I told her my predicament, and she didn't look at me as a failure. She was excited that I recognised the importance of ESOL, and she was happy that I realised my students were really ESOL students.

Mrs Bihari gave me a crash course in teaching ESOL. She loaned me some ESOL books for grammar exercises, and one Sunday afternoon she came to class to do a crash course in formal English verbs. Once again my bright, patient students trusted and followed me on my latest venture. I'm sure they wondered, "Is she ever going to get this right?"

Finally, I realised that nearly everything we did, grammatically speaking – even spelling-wise – had to have a comparative value. Students needed to compare formal English grammar and writing to Creole grammar and writing.

We went back to V.S. Naipaul's *Miguel Street* and examined Creole dialect juxtaposed with formal English narration. We went back to the diary of Christopher "Dudus" Coke and found commentary in formal English so that we could compare the two.

The mood changed drastically once my students realised they were second language speakers. Just like foreign language speakers whose first language was French or Spanish or German, they would often ask, "What is the word for this?" They might ask, "What verb should I use if I'm saying this?"

Stubborn problems – namely verb tenses – vanished quickly once we began to approach English from a second language point of view. It's amazing how quickly you can change the mood of a class. It's amazing how fast you can change the entire direction of a class once you are willing to make observations about why students are making certain errors.

There really is a solution for every problem. This is easy to say in hindsight. At the time, I was sweating bullets. Time was running out. Our CXC English language exam was around the corner and there was so much work to do. The good news was my students were reading more than ever, and writing book reviews.

Miguel Street *by V.S. Naipaul*
A Book Report

by Mark Friday

While reading Miguel Street, *I found myself sitting on the pavement alongside Hat, Edoes and Edward involving myself in their "ol' talk" and seeing, hearing and smelling the same things that they were experiencing.* Miguel Street *is captivating.*

Immediately, the author, V.S. Naipaul, shows you an amazing way how a change in environment could also change a person's behaviour and attitude. Bogart was quiet but – unfortunately for me, fortunately for him – he got a job on a ship and took an "extended leave." When he returned, his attitude was that of a foreigner – he even twisted his mouth and spoke like one. From being a quiet man who sat playing patience, Bogart began to smoke, drink and have big parties for the kids – even invite the gang over. Surprisingly, the change had nothing to do with his new job, but his new found status.

Aside from all the wonderfully placed characters of Miguel Street, I fell in love with two: Man-Man and Mr B. Wordsworth. Truly they are two completely different beings, but their opposite personalities are what kept me reading. Man-Man, said to be mad, uses his reputation to gather a crowd, but eventually comes to his senses, which also confirms that fact that he is truly insane.

B. Wordsworth, to me, deserved the title of "Mr". His calm and mystic movements not only capture the heart of the youth – whose name is never revealed – telling the story. Wordsworth was a poet and wonderful friend; it was sad how that chapter ended, but Mr B. Wordsworth will always be a part of my memories.

It is important to find yourself within the pages of a book: horror, informative, short story – any type of book – is worth it. Miguel Street does just that: It draws you in. Even if you are not in a cheerful mood, when you sit or lie down to read Miguel Street, you will, I guarantee, cheer up. V.S. Naipaul's Miguel Street blows even the most humourless souls on earth away.

Lost

It was raining hard, and YTC appeared deserted except for some disheveled lads with stunned frowns or smirks on their faces as they waited in line to process into the institution.

My students seemed a little down, but they fought their way through their plummeting emotions rather than withdrawing into themselves and pulling away from me.

Jahmai had just finished reading *The Lost World*. Marc Friday was reading *On Writing*, a guide to better writing, by Stephen King. Shawn and Marc had disappeared into their own writing during class. Sometimes, when they couldn't concentrate, they'd pour their feelings and fears in a letter or essay. Many of their essays expressed their utter dismay at any act of kindness. They didn't expect anything to be given to them – least of all kindness.

When they handed me essays they would say, "You always say we can write whatever we want, right, Miss?"

"Yes, because I will correct it for grammar and structure. No writing is ever wasted here," I said.

To pick up the mood, I suggested writing a poem about the ocean. Vaughn laughed and said, "I can't write a poem."

Most of the boys laughed and said, "No, miss, we can't write poems."

I said, "But you have to be able to write poems or you can't get a girlfriend."

They laughed like I was the funniest person in the world. They even tried to challenge me.

"No, Miss," said Ashton. "Girls like things. Fancy things: bling. "

"Money," said Peter. "Plenty money."

"Yes, they want you to give them expensive things," said Jahmai.

"The more the better," said Shawn.

Olton, always the romantic, always the optimist remained silent. I thought a trip to the ocean (at least in their minds) might be a welcome diversion. I was wrong. This was the only poem I got.

> *The Ocean*
>
> *By Marc Friday*
>
> *The whales, the sharks,*
> *The crabs, the seals*
> *The death, the pain,*
> *The secrets concealed*
> *The rage she feels*
> *The night she sees*
> *The world she holds*
> *The mouths she feeds*
> *The moonlight glitter,*
> *The sunshine's smile,*
> *The roar of my mother*
> *I'm the ocean's child.*

From a lad I'll call Abraham, I got a poem about love – not the ocean. Abraham popped up in class the day I tried in vain to get students to write that poem about the oceans. This happened from time to time. A lad who had already been registered for the CXC English language exam outside would find himself in trouble and in YTC. That was the case with Abraham. I made my mind up to have one more student especially after he settled right into class by writing a poem.

Love

By Abraham

Love is me love is you
Love is the thing that makes us two
Love is a feeling that flows in our heart
Loves is the sickness that tears us apart
Love is our darling, the one we hold dear
Loves is the disease in which we all fear
Love is the border that marks near the end
Love is the time in which we will spend
Love is the sight that shows us the way
Love is the might to go all the way
Love is the thought that's constant in our mind
Love is the sport we play every time.

While class was going on, Abraham suddenly got up and handed me a folded note. This was not unusual either. Abraham wrote:

Dear Miss,

This is not an essay. This is not a letter. This is just me asking for your assistance in order for me to at least get a pass in English. I understand almost everything you talk about or teach, the only thing that gives me problems is the essay.

I don't know why but I think I'll find out after this. Just for the record, I learn by physically doing things or if someone takes the time to explain it to me. I'm normally the type of person to sit and explain this to you, but it occurred to me that you like to read so I thought I would write instead or maybe I just thought you would better understand what I have to say if I write it.

I really like English and I really want to learn to write, but I can't without your help personally. I think that makes this the best thing I ever wrote apart from letters expressing my feelings to/for someone so please if you will fill in what's missing from this and get back to me I really need your help.

Abraham

Abraham seemed willing, but he had a difficult time settling in class. In that sense he was like Peter, who needed to move around to learn. But Abraham seemed to be doing more moving than learning.

What really got me was one preposition in that letter: "for". When Abraham wrote "I think that makes this the best thing I ever wrote apart from letters expressing my feelings to/for someone…," I realised that Abraham was probably one of the scribes in YTC.

There are many illiterate boys who depend on lads like Abraham to write letters for them. That is their only way to communicate with the outside world other than the two 15-minute visits they are allowed every week from family members.

I corrected Abraham's writing, which wasn't too bad, and I encouraged him to write more. Abraham's difficulty in writing mostly came from being so guarded. If you can't open up to write, and if your life is such a secret you can't show emotion, writing becomes very difficult – especially creative writing. Abraham became frustrated easily and he didn't take kindly to corrections. He wasn't willing to grind through difficult work as the rest were willing to do.

Still, I wasn't willing to give up. I hoped Abraham would settle into class.

One day we were doing some grammar exercises. As usual, you could hear a pin drop. Somehow my students had managed to figure out how to participate in class discussions and never interrupt each other. If someone wasn't answering a question, he remained silent.

Abraham came to class late as usual. He settled – as well as he ever settled – and gave excellent answers. I praised him, but he just looked angry.

I saw the moment when someone leaned over and whispered something to Abraham. Out came an explosive laugh.

"Hey, hey, you can stop holding class. Miss is the only person who holds class hear," shouted Kheelon.

In a split second, I realised Kheelon felt the need to defend me. I also realised the guard had left the room. Everyone jumped up to confront Abraham.

"Hey, hey, hey, you're all out of line," I said popping out of my seat.

Everyone sat down.

Abraham sulked. "I want to leave the class, Miss."

You could cut the tension with a knife.

"I think that is a wise thing to do, just walk away from the situation if you can't figure out how to control your feelings."

I thought Abraham would go outside to cool himself off, but he didn't come back. The guard returned and didn't seem to notice the tension. Every boy stared into my eyes and I could hear their silent pleas: Don't sell us out, Miss. The guard asked if Abraham had requested permission to leave class.

"Yes," I said.

In that moment, I realised just how quickly a fight could break out. I knew I hadn't handled the situation well. There just wasn't any time to think about what to do.

I lost Abraham that day. He never came back to class. Occasionally, I'd see him walking across the field.

"Please come back," I'd say.

He'd shake his head. "I just can't get that work," he replied.

"Yes, you can. You just have to stick it out."

He shrugged. "I'm not interested in writing the way they

want me to write. I want to do it my way," he said, and walked off.

Somewhere along the way, I thought, as I watched Abraham walk away, I failed this young man.

The White Wall

Personal essays poured in on top of all the creative writing and essays I assigned. I could count on extra writing from Marc.

Bad Boy

By Marc Friday

Human beings are funny people. That sentence sounds bad, but that sentence reflects us: we quickly correct others but never see the real mistake in ourselves. It is no lie, maybe – just maybe – there are really some people that care for others and are willing to give up their lives in order to prevent violence.

There are even those who say he was a bad boy and yes I was. But I was a bad boy with class and empathy. I knew the effect my actions would have on 'victims' but I chose to ignore those feelings and continue doing my thing. I didn't want to care; I didn't have time to care.

Times change, yes? And people change with time. Three years and ten months (the time I'm supposed to serve) is not really a long time, but it is enough time for your mind to develop and I'm sure it is enough time for your thinking capacity to become larger – I'm not sure if 'larger' is the correct word, but you know what I mean. If someone is given that amount of time to think about himself and how his decisions affect others, then hopefully, we might have two or three non-selfish people come out of a place like this.

We all sink or swim. The old lady in Titanic *– the Mrs who was the survivor – told the searching crew that: 1,500 people had perished that night, 20 boats were out there but only one turned back. Six people got saved after the Titanic went completely down. Six people out of 1,500, 20 boats that had half of the real weight and a bunch of first class idiots that were afraid to think. I hope that the person reading this is not afraid to think.*

Are you?

I had kept my promise about using the boring textbook for only about 20 per cent of the time, "…but we have to do some of the comprehension and writing exercises in there in case you get some of that boring stuff on an exam," I said.

One day, I saw a creative writing exercise that asked students to write a story that includes this line: "I stared at the ceiling, white and remote and at the wooden floor, cold and splintery under me."

"Let's tackle that," I said.

Everyone was game.

My Great Mistake

By Marc Friday

The people of Vessigny Village said I was a fool.

"Yeah! It good for him!" they shouted as I passed in a grey prison van, the smell pissy, the taste at the back of my throat, bitter like raw Aloe Vera slowly crawling her way down to my stomach. I had already accepted my fate: death or life imprisonment; I didn't care, I did my crime so I had to pay.

That was then. That was when Ratty-Boy told me that he would always have my back. I knew too many people on the yearly count of killings that took place in 2001 and with September 11 still fresh in people's memories, and my uncle, Mr Joe or Uncle J hooked on crack, my year began on the downside.

Ratty-boy and me were sent to the Maximum Security Prison in Arouca to begin our sentences. Ratty got 15 years for manslaughter and me, well let's say I got the defecation on my hand from holding the stick of fate. Life, why? Well Ratty kicked him down the steps and when he knocked out, I proceeded to stab him.

Now I sit on my bed looking at dead coloured walls – white – that dull light and make the room seem dead. I remember when they first put their filthy hands on me. They hit me all over my body causing me to sit in a cell in the Point Fortin police station and premeditate their demise. I lay there, I stared at the ceiling, white and remote, at the wooden floor cold and splintery under me the windows barred, the last closed door. The last closed door, blue. Blue bars and blue concrete to reflect the cold and distant relationship, a relationship that…

When you are taken out into the yard to do your left and right back and forth routine you will feel sick. Your eyes will fill with tears and your stomach will twist. The rest of your natural life will be spent in a yard with a wall so tall your eyes hurt looking up.

I killed a man and so what? Who cares? No one that's who. No one cares that I now spend my days in a place full of lunatics. The people I once embraced have forgotten me, left me to see these lifeless colours white, grey, dark blue. These walls, ceilings and doors – doors out of our reach, doors forbidden to our touch – we could get beaten half to death if you do – yet the temptation pinches our fingertips like frostbite on your fingers.

It's been 24 years since my condemnation, 24! 9 years since my chargee got out, I'm happy for him – kind of happy. I've seen many faces come in this powder-wall place, a place where we have to condescend; act as fools in order to live comfortable when I say fool I mean "fool".

I was 23 when I was convicted. Times changed, I changed with them. My hair has little grey strands now. My girlfriend is now a happily married wife and mother of three. Ratty-Boy got shot and killed by the police two years after his release. My mom passed so did my grandfather. At times I lay on my bed and looked up and spoke to the face on the ceiling made from dead mosquitoes and scraps, wet toilet paper that was once wet with some type of liquid now hard and dry.

I've spent more than half of my life in jail and I have experienced all kinds of pain. I've seen my fingers dead in front of me, unable to move an inch, my skin open like a purse, wide and red like the carpet at the Grammy Awards – if this were a movie I would get best actor and best director. I've heard the screams of inmates that get their manhood stolen. I've stabbed, I've sliced, I've saved myself from that.

Even though the pain in this place is great, nothing hurts more than that day when I was hit all over my body and placed in a cell premeditating the Point Fortin Police. I still remember when I stared at the ceiling, white and remote, at the wooden floor cold and splintery under me – the window barred and unreachable – the last closed door. Oh the last door closed.

The White Wall

By Jahmai

I stared at the ceiling, white and remote; at the wooden floor cold and splintery under me – the window barred and unreachable – the last door. It was happening all over again. Eva was escorting me down the aisle covered with rose petals.

"Go in and do your number," she said pushing me towards the lily white toilet bowl.

"Will you be waitin' for me?" I frighteningly asked for the millionth time because I did not want to be left on the altar again. After receiving the compulsory yes from her I went and took my place in front of the priest. After the usual five minutes of inactive stand, she led me back to my room passing other psychiatric patients.

My second shower had already passed and I could tell that there would be no more because the nurses were being paged every other second. Eva had started working here a month ago and she executed her duties very professionally, but today was just not one of her days. Lying on my bed, I asked her about the barred windows.

"Burglars," she still managed to answer before she left.

Fact was some months earlier a patient had jumped out of the 5th floor window. I wanted to be next because we could fly.

Buzz, Buzz, Buzz, I pressed the buzzer in vain because I was not getting an answer.

Where was Eva?

I moved to a corner of the room, seated myself and leaned my head against the padded wall. Buzz, buzz,

buzz, still no answer. The nurses on the night shift were all familiar with my game. That is what it was to them. Besides the ones who had put in years of service were the ones who couldn't care less about the patience.

Tonight I would not see Janice who is probably standing alone on the altar she and the priest both. Screaming at the top of my voice I use profane language at the nurses. When I grew too noisy, like a flash of lightening they're standing in front of me were two nurses (one male the other female) syringe in hand. They held me down and gave me a shot….

"Good morning, Mr Gibbs. Here is your breakfast." Small gentle hands were shaking him awake. After Ms Eva Goodridge had succeeded in waking me, she moved the curtain open, allowing the rays of sunlight to announce that a new day had started.

Janice my dearest, my heart has almost run cold, please take me to do a number, I begged. When she got me out of bed and we entered the corridor, I stared at the ceiling, white and remote and   the wooden floor cold and splintery under me – the window barred and unreachable – the last door. My wedding day is here.

Jahmai used his love for classics and a handout I had given him about the ancient Greek musician, Orpheus, to write a plea to Hades, King of the Underworld for the release of Orpheus's love Eurydice.

Song of Orpheus: To the Gate Keep of the Underworld

Oh great keeper of the underworld, so terrible you are not.

Truly respected and feared, but one's heart is not made of stone.

My cause remains the same, I am driven by love, the love

That has sealed me out of your palace of darkness.

My sounds should fill your heart with soft emotion, for not even the gods of Olympus can resist hearing my tunes.

Only you and you only, can help me retrieve what I've lost,

To the world you guard.

Think of me entering these gates as thyself gaining all that thou desires.

So enter may I please?

That I can regain what you guard so dearly from me for the second time.

Roller Coaster Ride

We watched Catfish. *The boys laughed nervously through the documentary exploding in peals of laughter once they realised how a homely woman had fooled the guy who had fallen in love with her by posing as a pretty woman whose identity she had stolen off the Internet.*

All right, I thought. That was weird.

From there, we analysed all the literary elements in "Now We Know" an article written by Jamaican author Roger Mais and published in the *Public Opinion* of Jamaica on July 14, 1944.

"He went to jail for six months for sedition because of that article," I said. "Sedition is what you get charged with if you're trying to incite mutiny and overthrow the government. Jamaica was still a British colony and the British used the British War Measures Act to charge him."

They didn't understand how Roger Mais could be thrown in jail for writing against the British.

"You really could go to jail for that?" asked Marc.

"Well, he did," I said.

The most interesting discussion came from "Defining White" a poem by Naomi Shihab Nye about a woman who is trying to define white based on a statement her photographer husband made about finding white light.

The last line says "Is wind a noun or a verb?" They wrote down their answers. Everyone – with the exception of Shawn – said wind was a noun and pronounced it wind as the wind that blows, but Shawn said wind like to wind up a toy.

They were lost. I tried to explain to them how that line showed prejudice and indeed made the reader engage in prejudice.

"It's not until we pronounce the word that we have to categorise it and decide if it's a noun or a verb. There on the paper, in its natural sense of existence it is neither. It's just a word."

They looked puzzled. They still have trouble with symbolism. Strangely enough, they have trouble using visual prompts for writing exercises as well.

When I gave them a picture of black and white people reacting to the verdict of the OJ Simpson trial, when OJ Simpson was found innocent of killing his wife, Nicole, and her friend, most of my students spoke about the black people's reactions in the picture and totally ignored the white people's reactions. I thought it might be because they could identify with the black people's reactions, but they said they realised the difference in reactions between the two races and thought it would be racial to talk about it.

I said, "But it is racial. The whole thing is racial. That is what the picture captures. "

Then I hit the jackpot: an essay entitled "Cool Like Me" by Donnel Alexander about black culture and the concept of cool.

This, I thought, should give them a sense of power because to discuss this essay they can go places I can't go. The article is filled with discussion of the "N" word, claimed and explained by the "cool" black guy in the article.

"I can't say the 'N' word," I explained. "Culturally speaking, I can't do it."

"It's just a word," they said, "used all kinds of ways."

"For you it has many meanings, for me, it's just a racist word."

The article also included figures of speech: irony, metaphors, puns, paradox, similes and French phrases.

Jahmai didn't have his copy of the essay with him, but he had his exercises.

I asked him, "Where's your paper, Jahmai?"

"Home," he said.

"Home?" I asked.

"That's a metaphor," Shawn said.

Even the guard on duty in the classroom said he was impressed with the lads' level of discussion – especially Jahmai's.

These were clearly the most left-brained, language-oriented young men I had ever known. Usually boys are so right-brained, so visually oriented. I always found boys did better using visual imagery and visual cues to create and form the structure of an essay, but not these young men.

Maybe, I thought, they need an artist to help them so I brought in Greer Jones-Woodham to teach them how to analyse a picture.

They picked out details in pictures that are barely noticeable and completely ignored the main point of the pictures.

After Mrs Jones-Woodham came to class, we looked at a picture in the textbooks of a traffic jam spread out over the meandering hills of San Fernando in southern Trinidad. Pedestrians are nonchalantly walking down the street and cars are backed up on the road.

Shawn wrote:

> *As all the other days on this street, cars are moving slowly, patrons are going about their own business. Everything seems normally busy, but for 32-year-old Michelle Mitchell the following takes place quickly and shockingly: She was sitting in the grey Mazda 626 when a pedestrian named Smith John, wearing long pants and T-shirt, walked up to her while sat in the front seat and snatched her purse. She held on tight on first extinct, but quickly let down her guard and lost the purse.*

The thief walked off while everyone was looking at him.

Only the guy in the shirt tried to stop him, however, he made a daring escape through the busy streets.

Smith John, who was caught one month after the incident, had walked down the hill with the look of terror in his brown eyes. The smell of alcohol was strong on him. Smith John was walking off with the purse when Ken, the guy in the shirt, looked at Tom, the African-American wearing the glasses and asked, "Did he just rob the woman?"

Tom said, "Yeah, but I not getting in that."

It was then Ken took off after Smith John and a heated fist fight ensued. Smith John pulled out a knife and stabbed Ken twice in his stomach. All the patrons rushed to Ken's assistance while Smith John escaped running through the traffic.

This is just a typical example of why Trinidad and Tobago has one of the highest crime rates in the world. Surely if both Ken and Tom had both gone after Smith John he wouldn't take out the two of them. But Tom was a coward so the perpetrator escaped with Ms Mitchell's purse, which, by the way, only had $8 and her makeup in it.

My jaw felt like it dropped to my knees. I could find no rhyme or reason for any crime scene in this picture. Anger, frustration, disappointment – any of the angst we get from a traffic jam, yes, but no crime.

"Hear what," I said after I read Shawn's essay, "you are all banned from choosing to write about any picture in the exam. Leave it. Don't do it. Don't touch it. Don't look at it. Stick with the writing prompts. You're good at those."

Back to the Drawing Board

Their descriptive essays came from their own experiences – as they should – but I wondered how the examiners would react to some of their rough imagery and their penchant for creating crime scenes in their stories. "Try not to scare people too much," I warned constantly, and they would laugh.

At the same time, I didn't want to censor them or make them feel like they shouldn't be finding a way to work through their experiences.

That's the difficulty with writing for an exam. It doesn't always measure life lessons: it only measures exam questions.

There are questions on the exam that relate to crime, but I bet those people sitting in an air-conditioned room with a pile of papers in front of them are not expecting the detailed descriptions these boys would give. So what are they expecting? Some make-believe crime story conjured up in students' heads?

And what of the questions about the place you grew up in or your favourite place to visit? How would my students deal with questions like those? They didn't want to deal with any prompts I gave them about a place outside of prison – like writing a poem about the ocean. It was almost as though they couldn't bear going to a place in their mind when their body couldn't follow. So they wrote about their place: prison.

YTC
by Shawn

It's no place to be. The sadness and loneliness of jail or a so called, "Correctional Institution". The way the officers treat the so called human beings like dogs, the sad look on each prisoner's face and the overall physical appearance of the place – it's all devastating and dilapidated.

Hearing the sound of an officer literally screaming at a prisoner, "Everyone up now!" and they coldly reply as if they don't have a choice, "Yes sir".

The smell of their clothes and body odours are terrible. You see them moving in a trance like everyone' eyes seem focused on something very distant. This is a symptom of being institutionalized. Listen carefully and you can hear, "Wap, wap, Wap!" This is the sound of an officer hitting an inmate with rapid strokes.

Every prisoner looks sad. If you were to talk to them, you would hear sadness in their voices. Their food tastes like something you would leave back for the dog. The whole situation is entirely out of place.

Physical appearance seems not to matter to them. How they live is a very negative, dominating factor. The walls that are supposed to be covered with paint are literally covered with graffiti. The stench is like a running sewer. You could only hear the distinct chattering of them inside the dorms. The bars blocking them from outside are rusty and you could see frustration.

It's no place to be as a visitor or inmate. It's straight out wrong. The place's main objective is supposed to be to hold and rehabilitate but it seems more to say by the description to capture and demoralize. Really no place anyone would ever aspire to reach.

We talked about structure in writing. Everything has a focus and a structure – even descriptive writing must have a focus.

"It can't just be about describing things. The descriptions have to come together to capture a theme," I said.

I told them if you wrote about each other and described each other only physically, you'd write basically the same thing.

They laughed. But I said, think about it. You all have short hair, the same clothes. You wear rubber slippers – no bling. How are you going to distinguish yourself from everyone else in here?"

We talked about describing a girl.

"How would you do that? Give me a word. Something you could build a theme around.

Ashton said, "Curvaceous," and I said, "That's good for about two lines and then you'll run out of things to say."

"Studious," said Jahmai.

Jahmai always gets it.

"And remember, I said, as much as possible, descriptive writing should cover all the senses: touch, sight, sound, taste and smell.

Kheelon's writing still had many issues with spelling and grammar, but he had good structure. Sometimes he could write two lines without making a mistake, and then it would become difficult to read a sentence that he had written.

"I think I know the problem, Miss," Kheelon said. "I think really fast, and I'm trying to keep up with my thoughts. I have to slow down a little."

"Half the battle is understanding your problem," I said.

They were all identifying their problems better. Marc knew he always had a problem with possessives; Shawn had a problem with capitalising proper nouns. They all leave words out sometimes.

Friday was writing a book and he said he felt he lost his literary voice in the last piece he wrote. He did. I told him it's not being dishonest to cut characters. There are too many people to keep track of and we can't have empathy for all. What is important are the events that impacted on the main character and there might be only a couple of characters he needs to reconstruct that.

"You don't have to recall every single detail, just what is important. Nonfiction requires a lot of editing in your mind. You have to edit out people and events that are insignificant," I said. "Sometimes the most difficult part of writing is knowing what to leave out – not what to put in. It's the same with life. We all have to learn how to self-edit."

The Cell Blocks

For a time, Jahmai seemed to have spent more time in the cell blocks than in the dorms. Often times, he found it easier to retreat to the cell blocks. Jahmai always wrote out his feelings. It seems he had written this inside the cell blocks, but held off giving it to me. I was struck by how Jahmai kept changing person, slipping among different pronouns in his three-part series on the cell blocks. That, I felt, said a lot about what he was able to face and what he had to distance himself from.

Part I: Cell block, friend or foe? Whether or not it qualifies as a friend or foe, it is the place where you are placed when you break the rules in jail. The cell block in YTC contains 20, 6' x 9' cells, six of which are separated from the others. Once you are housed in one of these six separated cells it is because you are considered to be a "High Risk Prisoner." To earn this title in YTC the authorities must be of the impression that one has a very volatile personality or is a perceived troublemaker. Either way the cell block is a place where people who are in trouble are kept.

Cell block, a friend – because one is housed in a cell by one's self, one is able to do some deep meditation and reflection. With all that's going on outside the cell block, meditation may be short lived. The cell block prisoners are left uninterrupted. They are privileged with two baths a day – morning and evening – and the only other interruptions that they face is when food is served or for church services.

This leaves prisoners with approximately 21 hours per day locked inside of their cells. Here you can *get some ability to focus, read books and studying doesn't seem to be a problem. Nelson Mandela was able to unleash his true potential by investing his time in reading when he was in the cell blocks. That allowed him to gain knowledge. Here he was able to change the way he viewed people.*

Take for another example Ex-Crip Gang Leader Tokie Williams. Mostly known for his gang-banging lifestyle "Tokie" was able to make a marvelous transformation in his life from the cell block. He wrote many motivational and education books as well as put a temporary end to the notorious Crips and Bloods gang war.

I'll even be bold enough to use myself as an example. Although I (Jahmai) have not sworn to my fullest potential or even close as a matter of fact, I continue to shock myself time and time again. I promised myself that the cell block wouldn't break me in any way.

I have changed the way I think. It has encouraged me to read. We – Mandela, Tokie and myself as well as a lot of others were able to make changes in our lives that needed to be changed. We were given a second chance through prison because we weren't killed so we reframed our minds for the better from the cell block.

Part 2: Cell block, as a foe! Lonely as ever. Most of the time prisoners are caught up in their own problems so most of the day you could hear a pin drop. In such a state of dwelling it's hard to tell that anyone else exists; yet sometimes it is the total opposite. When the prisoners start making a ruckus, it is really hard to hear yourself, but this hardly happens, kind of like once every blue moon. To bring more light to what I'm saying – to be more precise – the prisoners who partake in the ruckus are the one's who consider the cell block to be a foe.

Those who view the cell block as a foe are for most of the time angry or emotionally traumatised – angry because they take the experience as a setback in the process of "rehabilitation." They don't utilize their time to make a positive difference. They carry the misconception that once they are confined to the cell block they are supposed to be "monsters" and what better way to convince themselves than to banish all their emotions except anger.

Those who become emotionally traumatised are the ones who fall victim (prey) to the hands of the "monster" (predator). These "monsters" taunt and beat the preys to keep them in their frightened lost state of mind, so when asked to fulfill unmanly tasks for them they comply every time. Becoming emotionally traumatised happens when the cell block lands its best punches right in your face and you are knocked out. The loneliness, the unmanaged wasted hours and living in eternal regret all create an emotionally traumatised person.

Then there is the punishment that one must initially face upon entry to the cell block. One does not find himself in the cell block unless an offence is committed that violates prison policy. Punishment ranges from: rationed diets to strokes. These all determine whether you become a "monster". It all depends on how one chooses to view one's punishment – either as fair or unfair.

So is the cell block a friend or a foe? It all depends on how you view the given circumstances. All this I have faced yet I have conquered them all. Amazingly extraordinary how even in a supposedly bad situation much good can still emerge. It all depends on how you view a situation.

Cell block, neither a friend or a foe. It is just another part of a prison.

The Poets of QTC

"Sometimes, you just have to suck it up," I said. We were talking about poetry. After my attempt to get them to write about the ocean failed, I shelved the idea of writing poetry, but I wasn't going to give up.

"You can't understand poetry and write essays about poetry if you can't write poetry," I said.

"If you want to get girlfriends –"

"Oh no, Miss, you said that already," they laughed and tried to wave me off.

"And we told you girls want guys who have money and things to give them," said Ashton and Shawn. "Girls want clothes and cell phones. Nice things. Lots of things," they said.

So the battle positions had not shifted. Since my first attempt to get them to write poetry, most of my students had written about the pressures they had felt to come up with lavish gifts for girls when they were outside of the institution.

"Clearly, you are not meeting the right type of girls," I said. "The girls I know would love to have poems written for them. That's the type of girl you have to look for when you get out of here."

Finally Vaughn, always willing to try anything, said, "I'll support you, Miss."

"Me too," said Olton.

"I write poetry," said Marc, and everyone groaned.

And there was another willing participant, JR, one of the original 27 students who went out for a work programme, but came to class when he could. He happened to be in class the day I announced we'd tackle poetry again, and he was game. He would come to Mr Taylor's class, he said, because it was on a Sunday and he didn't have to work. I had always hoped JR would stay. He had a lot of potential, but given the choice between going out to work and taking your chances on a CXC exam seemed to be no choice for most lads. They'd opt for the job every time.

"The good news is that a real poet is going to teach you to write poetry."

Writing poetry is not my forte, so I asked Mervyn Taylor to teach that lesson. Mervyn is a retired English teacher who taught in challenging inner-city New York schools. He has published several books of poetry, and he's one of my favourite poets.

The "lads" were subdued and guarded when Mervyn came to class. Jahmai sent a message he felt sick, and he couldn't come to class. I sent a message back that I would come inside their "dorms" and get him.

Reluctantly, Jahmai came, but he would not look at me for the entire class. Shawn turned away from Mervyn for the entire class. I decided not to push him. Kheelon kept chewing on the inside of his mouth and glancing at me. Kheelon had secretly confessed that he wanted to write poetry because he had been reading a book of Tupac Shakur's lyrics. Mervyn asked them to write poems about home. They stared in the distance dreamily but perked up when he said, "Then you're going to write an erotic poem without being sexually graphic."

So they wrote:

I Met Her Once

by Marc

I met her once
By a store watching a pair of shoes,
"Good afternoon" I greeted,

"Hi" she replied,
My heart raced
She answered, she did.
"Are you buying those?
"Nah I just eyeing them;
"They're nice, huh?"
"Yeah. They would look good with my dress."
"White dress?"
"Baby blue"
"Cool"
We hit it off,
Names exchanged;
Numbers passed
Now I'm here
3 months, 7 days after.
She's looking at me writing
"That your diary?" she asked.
"Yeah" I replied
"Write down it was fantastic."
It was fantastic!
I met her once,
I loved her ever since.

Heaven

by Jahmai

The bright paint on the walls,
Overpowers your sense of time
Inside the walls, Christmas never ends
The pictures on the walls are no strangers,
There is a new one that represents
someone vulnerable to danger
The spirits of the people are like cats,
pleasant, but innocently mischievous.
The queen in this place is the one who does all the
hard work; she washes and cooks and sees
about us all, she is worshipped and adored,

Picturing a place like this without rest,
gives the impression that here will be tiring
But here you can find comfortable rest.
The rooms are warm, and the beds are cozy
In this heaven,
so just like kings and queens, we sleep royally.
In the morning, noon and night, any
hunger can be satisfied. With food of all kinds,
coming from a place smelling like a bakery
and fine restaurants combined.
Welcome to my home.

I Live

by Olton

I live in a place
That has 2 lifestyles
The gangster life where
They rob and kill people
And the good life
Where people care and love each other
A place where you can hear the breeze passing by
And smell an unknown person's meal
from right around the corner
Church choirs sing loud until heaven comes down
Different avenues and different streets
Where careers build and talents soar
You will bounce into those
Whose lives are like a blank, crumpled up paper
Waiting to be discarded
You may have heard the name before
But not what's in it
Only I know because that's where I live
Sweet Malabar

Dirty Little Secrets!

by Jahmai

Don't say another word,
Gesturing with my hands
Exactly what I mean.
Giggling slightly, she
Holds me close,
Pressing her nakedness against my bare body
Afraid she surely is not
She craves that breath-taking feeling yet again,
Her hardened points are telling me all,
Her dirty little secrets.
The magic between us always starts off slowly-until
The dark magician in her breaks free-
And ends in a rush when the passion
Forces us to let ourselves go.

Love Stinks

by JR

She sliced through my heart like an orange
I gave her someone with love and kindness
In return I got a monster
How can an angel lie?
I ask myself that question every day
I know the answer to my question
But still I poison myself with these lies
How can an angel lie?
Trust is fundamental for any relationship
I trusted her but she did not trust me
I loved her more than I love myself
now she's moved on and I am still in
the same place
like a baby now learning to walk life moving
no, love stinks.

During poetry class Marc wrote the following:

By Marc

My father's father was my identical twin – or I was his since he's older – but we never saw eye to eye. His father was a lion of a man, but in those days when you misbehave you get it, and good too! Those beatings did something to him. They spoke to him and said, "Hey prince, beat your kid!" or "Don't cry sissy!"

My grandfather was no sissy; neither was he a girl – he had the kids to prove it – to anyone in our village I was his first grandchild, but the least loved. Our fights were spectacular. Wonderfully orchestrated! We fought because I wanted, but he only showed love by his wife and his mother. Then again when you think about how he grew up and his "feeling restriction" who could blame him. I love him, ha! Only I do.

Jahmai knocked out an extra poem:

The Hand
Jahmai Alton Donaldson

Why rough hands, why?
After the screams slapped your ears,
A little one dies.
Hard, strong and calloused you are,
You cause numbers to gather from afar.
Strike after strike, now causing me
To struggle, fight; even scream
But you conquer your worst fear
By holding my mouth, so the neighbours won't hear.
Day after day it happens to me,
But I dare not tell anyone,
For I fear to be found drifting under the sea.
Stinging as it feels, landing across my face,
I just rub grease on it and feel not disgraced.

Day after Day it happened, no one could have saved me,
My greatest fear has now ended,
I am drifting under the sea.

When class ended, they smiled – a different smile from the initial nervous ones. These smiles conveyed relief and the happiness that comes from reaching deep inside and discovering something new – like love or the meaning of home.

An Outing Gone Bad

Nothing ever happens the way you imagine it to be or the way you plan it. The perfect outing – or at least what you planned to be a perfect outing – turns into a nightmare, but even in a nightmare there are a few glimpses of hope, a few bright spots to focus on in all the turmoil.

I really looked forward to our field trip to see the Secondary Schools' production of *West Side Story*.

Nothing about that field trip went well. The bus bringing the lads to town came late. We sat in the back of the auditorium set apart from everyone like lepers. Our backs against the wall, the aisle to our right and two empty rows of seats in front of us served as our boundaries, cordoning us off from the rest of the patrons.

"Did you notice how they isolated us from everyone?" asked Vaughn.

Kheelon expressed everyone's shock when he asked, "Are they going to sing through the whole play?" With the exception of Shawn, no one had ever been to a musical.

Still, it was an outing, time away from YTC, a pleasant diversion until we ended up waiting and waiting and waiting for the bus to arrive. The play had finished by 1:00 p.m. The boys were busy checking out other students.

"We want to see other secondary students," they said so they stood there, gripping the rails, trying to figure out all the different school uniforms. Eventually the hall emptied. Nothing remained but the hollow echo of our own voices. We sat down on a bench.

Cleaners mopped around our raised feet and finally moved us downstairs to the lobby. Jahmai entertained himself by looking outside.

"Look at that girl walking across the street and coming towards us; walking like she's alone on a catwalk," said Jahmai.

Swinging her arms and hips like a confident model, she turned abruptly and disappeared among the vendors.

"I try to talk to people, but I find myself just saying things they want me to say," Jahmai said when we sat down again.

He's worried about disappointing everyone – including himself.

"I want to do everything right. I realise life is a marathon – not a sprint. I have to take things slowly."

We missed Marc, who managed to miss the event because he got sent to lockdown. Jahmai slid slowly into one of his dark moods.

"Everything works well in lockdown," said Jahmai. "I'm by myself and I think and when I'm out in the dorms there are distractions."

"But lockdown is not a good place," I said.

"I know," said Jahmai, and I could feel the sadness in his voice.

The clock ticked on: 2:00 p.m., 3:00 p.m., 4:00 p.m.

Hungry and tired they soldiered on.

"I never thought I would be so happy to get back to YTC," said Shawn.

How tall do you think you feel when, at the end of a field trip, teenagers from prison tell you they wish they were back inside their prison? I felt like an utter failure.

Feeling more like a bear foraging for her cubs than a teacher, I left the boys to buy something for them to eat from the vendors outside. Armed with orange juice, cheese biscuits, peanuts and homemade sweet bread, which the vendors helped me carry because the boys couldn't come outside – not even with a guard – I returned to the slumping, yawning, frowning boys.

About 5:00 p.m., the bus came. I went home disappointed.

Much to my surprise, they weren't damaged by that fiasco of an outing to see *West Side Story*.   When I returned to class the next week, my students wanted to know when we could go to another outing.

Shawn and Jahmai gave me essays about the experience.

An Outing Gone Bad

by Shawn

An exciting experience was an outing courtesy Ms Debbie Jacob, my English teacher, to the National Academy of Performing Arts (NAPA) to watch the musical Westside Story. *An exciting experience involved arriving late. We actually watched the play, and the grand experience was leaving four hours after the play finished.*

We were supposed to leave YTC at 8:30 am. We were on our way at 10 am. When we arrived it was already late and the play had begun. We used the first entrance. It was really dark, and I couldn't even see the stairs; however, I could hear the excitement in the voices of the actors and the seemingly very young crowd, mostly primary level school children.

We didn't miss much of the play, which was about two gangs living in America, one Puerto Rican and the other Americans. They were fighting for turf. Maria, the Puerto Rican girl, falls in love with Tony, an American boy. They keep their relationship low. There is a rumble, people are killed. The play ends in unity.

The irony is that YTC and the people associated with the prison are supposed to be most disciplined at all times, but YTC seems to have a disciplinary problem when it comes to being on time. Four hours after the play had finished, we were still at NAPA waiting on our bus. Ms.Jacob was kind enough to make the long wait with us and even buy food stuff for us. She didn't get anything for the guards.

Over all, I enjoyed the outing and without thinking twice I'd go to one any time it comes around again. Even with the long wait to leave, I enjoyed my time away from incarceration. I know our problems were totally out of Ms's control and I would like to ask her to please stop taking blame for them.

"I want you to stop apologising for things that are not your fault. Don't take the blame for things that are out of your control," Shawn told me the day he handed me the essay. "You do it all the time," he said.

From that day on, Shawn kept on my case about apologising for other people's behaviour or actions. It was a habit I had to break, and Shawn was determined to break it.

Bitter but Sweet

by Jahmai Donaldson

Every good experience leaves us with an even better story to tell. On Thursday, last, I, along with some other students, was given the opportunity to visit the National Academy of Performing Arts (NAPA) for the first time. Also to add to our blessing, we were fortunate to witness a musical – West Side Story. After an awakening performance with wonderful singing – especially from the lead actors – the play finished and it was time to leave, just as everyone else, except for the staff. One would think that our experience was over, but guess what?

After we made our way out of the auditorium, I asked our supervisors for a bathroom break before we hit the road; I was granted permission. When I returned, upstairs was free from wandering feet and the only people in sight were my classmates, teacher and supervisors. I would now be informed that our transport would be running a little late. This to me was really ironic given the fact that my classmates and I are prisoners; one might think that one would not want us lingering in the capital without proper and sufficient supervision. (There were six guards with us). Anyhow, I was happy because I was in no rush to return to prison.

Sight-seeing from our position did not allow us to see much. We were mostly "bird-watching" until some of us sat down for a fruitful conversation with our teacher. Time passed, a lot was discussed and learned and we were called downstairs. Thinking that it was time to go, we came downstairs only to find out that we had more waiting to do but in a more exposed space.

I personally started feeling embarrassed because here we were being ushered in the direction of the door. If it were not for my teacher's status, I would have literally died because I am not accustomed to being publicly embarrassed.

We all sat once again to devour the fruitful conversations and lessons that our teacher was serving. In the corner of my eyes I noticed a boy mopping the floor and coming in our direction. I thought to myself, "Please don't allow him to reach us before we leave." I also made mention to some others about the feeling of embarrassment in my head and they all had the same feeling.

When my worst feeling was about to come to pass, our torturer decided to take a break with his mop. Thank God. By this time I guessed what was on everyone's mind was, "Where the hell is the bus?"

Any passersby would think that we were having the time of our lives, and probably we were. I mean we were laughing our heads off at our own misery.

Someone said, "We are probably looking like bums because hours after the show we were still in these people's place." We were making it through our misery with smiling faces and Miss stood fast right here with us although she, my new comrade, could have gone and left us there.

When we were forced to change locations once again, this time being ushered to a place not so visible, our new comrade set out to find us something to eat because we did not eat since about 7 a.m. and it was now after 4 p.m.

I think we would have all showed our true colours if Miss had deserted us, but she didn't. She stuck with us there and suffered with us. Just when she returned with food and saved the day, the transport arrived to take us back to prison. Well I guess the moral of this story is, you can get through any situation and not live to regret it once you are surrounded by people willing to share the pain with you so the burden would not seem too unbearable. Thanks Miss, for a great story of my own.

The main concern for all my students – and anyone in YTC – was not to be abandoned.

I had considered that field trip to be a dismal failure. It turned out to be the best thing that happened to us. After that day, we all felt closer to each other: we had stood beside each other and we could count on one another. It wasn't a big deal in the scheme of things. Being left behind to wait for four hours isn't an earth shattering event, but it was a symbolic one.

Everyone seemed to open up more after that day. Soon after, Shawn shared an important glimpse of his life.

A Broken Promise

by Shawn

As a young boy, I wasn't the most loving person. I stole from my parents; I ran away from home to visit the beaches and hunt. And I was always getting into trouble with our fellow neighbours, shooting at their latrines with catapults and other mean things.

Between the ages of eight to 12, I was probably just another kid, but I distressed my household, stealing money to buy bike parts and snacks and even fighting with all my siblings.

For years everyone tried to figure out why I behaved in such a violent manner, why I never listened, why I used to stay away from home all day. No one could figure me out. But I always knew why. I distressed over my parents' separation. I never settled down and I even went to jail at age 16.

See, as a kid, I remember walking the streets with my mom and my dad. Wind couldn't blow between them for they were so close. One night I looked up at them and asked, "Mom, can you and dad make a promise?"

"What is it, son?" my mom replied.

I said, "Promise me that you and dad will always stay together."

"We promise," they simultaneously answered.

It was a complete three years before they broke that promise. After that I decided that I would by all means necessary make my parents feel my pain so I always did things in both their neighbourhoods to stain their names.

That outing would lead to many more revelations and many more confessions.

Facing Fear

Kheelon once said, "There is no happiness in here. You have to find your own happiness." YTC was a place where you also had to face your fears. I was no exception.

One day, I was sitting in the visitor's room, waiting for a guard to take me to the school when I overheard an inmate complaining about something that I quickly tried to put out of my mind.

The inmate had just walked away when Miguel, from Maximum Security Prison arrived in the green prison bus with his assigned guard. Miguel had been coming for the last five months of my CXC English language class because he had a pack of CXC passes, but he had failed the CXC English language exam twice before.

We began to walk across the grounds to the school.

Miguel's guard decided to stop off in the administration building. "Stay here," he said, "until I get back."

A lad from YTC, who was cutting the grass, came across to talk to Miguel.

"I have five more months," he said to Miguel.

"That time will go fast," said Miguel.

"No it won't," the boy said. "That's a long time."

I stood there under the shed, listening to the two boys talking, and suddenly, as the guard was just about to go inside the administration building, I shouted, "I don't want to stay here. I'm afraid."

Miguel and the boy gasped and took a step backwards. The guard came running towards me.

"What happened?" the guard asked.

"When I was in the waiting room, a young man cutting the grass came quarrelling to the guards and said, 'I can't cut the grass anymore. I have told you all for the longest while it is infested with caimans inside here. There are baby caimans running in the drains now and there are caimans all over the place.'"

Miguel's horrified face – no doubt from the feeling I had tried to get him in trouble, morphed into a warm smile. He took a step towards me.

"Don't worry, Miss," Miguel said. "I'll watch out for the caimans."

"There's no caimans in the drains," the guard said.

"I don't know about that," I said.

Of course this was the hot topic in class when Miguel gave his report.

"Miss, you afraid of caimans? The caimans are over in the lake way in the back where the tracker dogs are," said Ashton.

"The lake? The same place where Ms McDonald said we could go to have class?"

"Yes, Miss, the same lake. The caimans will run from us."

Kheelon said, "There really are a lot of caimans around here. Sometimes we catch them and eat them."

"Are you all crazy?" I said. "They're endangered species. You can't eat them."

"But they come inside our place," said Kheelon.

I shook my head. "So if you trespass in someone's yard, do they have a right to eat you?"

"No that's different. We're people."

"I don't want to meet any caimans," I said.

Kheelon and Miguel – any of my students for that matter – made a point of being as chivalrous as possible after that day.

"Follow me, Miss," they'd say when we crossed the grounds to or from the school. "I'll go ahead of you to watch for caimans."

Eventually I would confront my fear of caimans. After the CXC exam was over, I asked one day to go by the lake to have class.

Surrounded by tall trees with singing birds and golden butterflies, the lake in back of YTC captured the remote marshlands of Caroni or Nariva.

We sat there on the benches while the boys kept a constant vigil for caimans.

"I love it here," Ralph said. Ralph, a young man in remand, had joined us to work on the CXC English literature exam. "I never knew a place like this existed in Trinidad."

"Look over there!" the boys shouted and pointed to the middle of the lake.

There, swimming towards us were a couple of pairs of eyes, one belonging to a caiman; the other to a turtle. Slowly, but surely, they swam through the lake creating a path of rippling water.

We all watched in amazement.

"I hope I don't have to run for my life," I said.

"Don't worry, the boys said. "We're here. We'll protect you Miss."

Ralph later wrote about that lake.

My Favourite Place in the World

By Ralph

In the most recent years while being here in YTC, I have discovered a fantastic place, that is the lake. The very sight of it is breath-taking. It's wide, full of dark-green water reflecting off the huge bamboo trees towering over the river and lake. The smell of fresh river water blending with the lake and the variety of plants and fish life overwhelm your nostrils with nature's best.

It feels almost heavenly as the cold rush of breeze and wind cut through your skin like never before. You can hear the birds flying overhead and hear them darting into the water.

Splash!

They raise up to flight again as they hunt for fish food for their babies. It's like a picture from a movie. It's a place I'd like to be everyday just to marry my time with nature's finger.

Somewhere along the way I lost my fear of caimans.

Letters

In this push-button age of instant messaging, social networking and e-mails, correspondence is something that is knocked out at a blistering pace. There's no time to think about messages stripped to acronyms like OMG or LOL.

We take communication for granted. Not since I first arrived in Trinidad and Tobago nearly 30 years ago, had I felt the joy of reading a long, handwritten letter. When I first came to Trinidad and Tobago, I would anxiously walk to the post office in Caroni every day, hoping to get one of those thin, blue aerogrammes. When no aerogramme came, I sadly walked home. The wait made any letter feel special.

The boys wrote many letters, some to me, some to teachers who had given them books. Ashton slipped a letter to me on Mother's Day:

> *You come here every week – even on Mother's Day – and never let us down, Miss. We know you should be home with your family today, and we are honoured that you have chosen to be with us. We don't forget such acts of kindness.*

I looked forward to my letters in YTC, and I took great care to write letters back to my students.

One day it occurred to me that I should tell my students that all of those novels I gave them every week actually came from the kind donations of teachers in my school or fundraising events students held. Sometimes people outside of the school gave me money for books.

My students decided to write letters to the teachers. This was Jahmai's letter:

Dear Teachers,

At one point once in my life I could have cared less about achieving anything that revolved around academics. One could say that I was a lost case and most did. I too thought so. I was so lost that I got involved in violent crimes, and now I am incarcerated at the Youth Training Centre. I was still racing on the highway of lost hopes – even in my incarceration. It was not until I was fortunate enough to be a part of Ms Jacob's English class, that my opinion started to change.

Whenever she stepped into the classroom, all stern faces would immediately transform into faces full of happiness. She had the kind of charisma that you could not resist, and to top things off she always knew how to address each individual in a witty, yet uplifting way. Saturday after Saturday she comes bearing books for us. I personally thought that she had a heart of gold along with a boat load of money to be purchasing brand new books every Saturday for us. It was only last class that I truly heard that the books are purchased, but with the assistance of the teachers of International School of Port of Spain. They donate money to buy books for the lost souls, no they donate books to help educate and recover lost souls.

Recently Ms Jacob had the class analyse the quote "Not everybody is healthy enough to love somebody." I now personally believe that the teachers of the International School of Port of Spain are the healthiest people in the world. You all are truly generous, seeking the interest of total strangers sure takes a lot of love; we really appreciate you all for your generosity. The only way I see it fit to repay you all is to read all of the books that are given to me; take care of them; be grateful of course because we are not just anybody being assisted.

We are prisoners; trying to acquire at least half of your health so my bitter and ill hearted ways are behind me forever. I could go on and on expressing my gratitude, but all things must come to an end. However, what I do wish could last forever is this hopeful and uplifting spirit inside of me that you all and Ms Jacob have given me. Thank you all, probably unknowing, you all have saved a life.

I didn't know what to say to Jahmai so I wrote him a letter.

Dear Jahmai,

I once bought a gold-rimmed china tea cup decorated with violets for a secretary I worked with at Boeing Commercial Airplane company in Seattle. She cried when I gave it to her and said, "No one ever thought of associating me with something so beautiful and delicate as a china tea cup."

I had given Gloria that tea cup after a good friend of mine, who was trying to lift me out of a blue funk, suggested that I deal with sorrow by giving. It worked.

Over the years, when I seemed to become poorer economically speaking, but richer in spirit, I figured out that giving meant more than presents. It meant a kind word, some praise – simple things that people didn't expect in a day.

When I came to YTC, I could give time and books and the knowledge I have learned from those books. I could organise ways to buy books, and that gave me a healthy dose of humility – something we all need.

What I never bargained for, Jahmai, was to have a class of such special young men, a class in which you stand out for your wit and voice; intelligence and kindness. I wish that I could give you half of what you have given me since I came to YTC. I know that you are anxious to get out in the world and experience so much – including love.

 When I was young, I wanted someone to love me more than anything in the world. Many years of disappointment made me realise that the love we all seek must come from within. While we're waiting and hoping for a better future, we have to find solace from inside ourselves.

That's where all of our love comes from – even our love for God. I have come to a point in my life where all I want is hope – for a better world; hope for a better future; hope for the young people of this nation; hope for you.

You are such a special young man, Jahmai with a wonderful spirit. You are the epitome of perseverance. I was touched when you wrote a thank you letter to the teachers in my school who have so generously supported you and described me as someone with "charisma."

 I am almost 58 years old and no one ever described me as having charisma.

Sincerely,
Miss

  Sometimes I wrote letters to keep my students motivated during the week while I was gone – at least that is what I told myself.

Dear Olton,

There isn't a day that goes by without me remembering the first paragraph you wrote for me in English class.

I knew from that one paragraph about wanting to be a turtle that you had to be in my English class no matter what. You were the first student to make an impression on me because your response to that writing prompt was so creative and so unusual.

Even now, when you write, there is always something that is so touching and real; unusual and insightful. I loved your poem about Malabar as well. I could really feel the beauty and the horror of the place.

You are such a bright young man, Olton, with an amazing future ahead of you. I love how you have a name that suggests a wise, old soul inside a young man's body. I love your optimism, your smile, your upbeat personality, your wry sense of humour and simple spirit, your dedication to whatever you do. You always look ahead and plan for the day you have a wife and children, and that is admirable.

We have a lot of work to do to get the mechanics of writing down, but that will come. The more you write, the better you will become so try to write as much as you can for me. Try letters, stories, descriptive writing, poems – short pieces. Don't forget to keep reading, and applying the lessons from *Uncommon*.

Keep working hard, and never give up. I believe in you.

Sincerely,
Miss

"That's a good letter," Olton said, as he carefully folded up his letter and slipped it back in his envelope. "I'm going to read it again. Many times. I am going to keep this letter for a very long time."

Callaloo and Me

Strangely enough, I can't recall exactly when the stories of their lives came pouring out in amazing detail. They could have come just before the exam or right after. Somehow, they came with a flurry of feelings.

Callaloo and Me

by Jahmai

Callaloo – a dish resembling soup, but green in colour; comprised of ochroes, dasheen bush, coconut milk – is the simplest example I can use to describe my life before incarceration. A little of everything both positive and negative. I was born and raised in south Trinidad – San Fernando – for most of my juvenile years until I started exploring the rest of the island with "bad company."

I came from a single parent household where my mother was the head of the house and had to provide for her nine children. We – the children – did not all share the same house but were still much inspiration to one another. Financially we were not well grounded, but we were rich in values: moral values.

The house that I lived in was well kept. The bills were handled behind my back. I knew there were bills that were being paid because I was mature enough to know that one needs money to survive in a material world. As I was supplied with needs mostly and not so much wants, I developed an attitude to "make do" with whatever I was awarded. Reading this passage one would make a clear observation that my family is the first and most appreciated possession of mine.

I found most of my companionship in my family not so much in friends. My friends always seemed to have something extra that I didn't have. Whether it was: cable TV, TV on the whole, parents with vehicles, nice clothes and shoes or bikes they had it I didn't.

I noticed that most of the extra they had was material things. For this reason I felt more comfortable around my brothers and sisters because they were in the same position as I was in financially. One thing I was always proud of was that they (siblings) were all extremely smart – myself included. If only I valued being smart for the long term effect instead of as a temporary asset of mine that I could have boasted with because I was so far ahead of my peers academically.

After I wrote my SEA in primary school I passed for a good school. Everyone thought that I would have been the next sibling on the road to academic success, but I suddenly didn't value what I possessed any more. I was always viewed by my peers as a genius compared to them, and I didn't want to care what my new school mates thought about me because I was already accepted by so many.

What finally changed life for me as I knew it was when I moved out of my home and into another place. Then I was the only sibling other than my little sister. I was now turning 13 and I developed a more keen sense of my appearance. Now I had a greater interest in girls and I was surrounded by the more shallow ones who were interested in mostly vanity. Those were the ones I went for.

Now that I was even more aware of my financial position – because the move from a concrete house to wood helped to shed some light on the financial *position of my mother – I seldom asked my mother for anything. This is when the so called "bad company" came into my life.*

My mother worked in Port-of-Spain, and I started to lose respect and interest in my older siblings because I now viewed myself as different from them. I was now the holder of much more unsupervised time. It was in this time I started to smoke and hang out with the neighbourhood drug dealer.

At the time it didn't seem so dangerous because no one in the area was afraid of him and people spoke highly of him – even the residents who were not involved in any kind of crime. The more my mother spoke to me, the more I grew distant from her.

She made me feel all emotional and I didn't want that feeling because none of my friends had any – at least out in public. I stuck myself in between two emotions: love and anger. If ever I was sad or disappointed I classed the feeling under anger, anything else would classify as happiness, even if it was pain, as long as no one I liked was the one in pain. If the person in pain was someone I liked then I would be angry, not sad not hurt.

The first crime I committed was not against any law but against myself. I never viewed my change in priority as a defeating one. I viewed it as the new me. This new me was determined to get what I wanted, made not to care about anyone except family and at any means try to hurt them – family. This meant that I had to be the new me behind closed doors.

This new me was fuelled by vanity. With my first girlfriend being one of the shallowest persons in the world, things only got worse. Also, by me not setting a standard for myself clearly said that I was quite shallow, just at the time I would not dare think that about myself.

There were countless attempts to bring me back to my original self by concerned relatives – especially my mother – new friends, girlfriends who grew up with moral values, but I kept telling myself that nothing was wrong with me that doing petty crimes was just how I choose to make money. Have you ever been there, ignorant and in denial? Heeding the advice of my criminal friends made me more comfortable in the doomed bed I was making for myself.

I cheated my way out of what I thought was a bad situation and found myself so much further in a worse situations – crimes that paid.

My decisions at that time, I wanted to believe, came on as a result of my own desire and my own decisions, but looking back I was indeed fueled by most of my peers because my mother was working an underpaying job to pay for our expenditures. Most of my friends, far older than me, became the most influential people in my life because my mother was working long hours and I really wasn't close to my siblings any more. I thought my friends came from the same type of family that I did except that they did not look financially exhausted.

They had nice clothes, nice shoes, gold chains. Unlike me, they weren't getting attention for being poor. I wanted that desperately for my outlook to change. I felt people looked at me and felt I was poor. The school I attended was not about who was bright or who was not bright. Everybody there got into that school because they were bright. At my school, it was about who had and who didn't have: things, I mean.

I had setbacks financially, and I had to deal with pulling and tugging from friends and family in directions they wanted me in. I knew the difference between right and wrong. I felt I had a choice. I thought my options were limited. I needed to make a decision. Now, I was fed up. I could have either listened to my mother with her advice about praying for a better tomorrow and waiting for God to take over or take up the advice given to me by peers, which was selling some weed.

When you're a child, you're vulnerable to adult predators who may have their own personal reasons for exploiting a child. The mind is impressionable and I was basically alone. There was a gang of us. The older ones have the say. No one tried to override the oldest person in the group who was about 28 at the time.

Eventually I began doing more and more crimes, and they became more serious. As time went on I wanted more: more things, more attention, and so you keep escalating to a next level, bigger crimes because of greed and wanting more and thinking it would all last forever.

Living under my mother's roof soon was not an option. The money that roamed outside of her doors that never slept was all that flooded my thoughts.

At about 15, I chose not to be around my mother. I had to because her wishes for my life weren't the same. Actually we both wanted the same thing for me – a good life – but we both had different ideas about how I should get that. A good life for me was the one I was living. I had all the petty things that 15 year olds want and more, money was not the problem. Discipline, values and respect were the problem. I thought I was helping people out.

The truth was I probably helped everyone who really didn't care what I became. Everyone who wanted me out of the life I was living never accepted any gifts from me, yet they still showed genuine interest in my well-being. However crime never stopped until I was brought to YTC. That's my life in a nut shell. Unlike many youths who took part in sports, I chose chaos.

My First Night in YTC – Marc Friday

I never pictured myself in a place as confining as this: YTC, a house of horrors where ghouls and zombies attack every good and honest part of a young delinquent's life. I remember my first night, but not like yesterday. I remember the fear and hate inside of me; I remember my fists clenched and both arms around Monkey-man and Pipie's shoulders, with a bloody arm and a hole the size of Alaska in my ankle.

Hah! It's funny when I look back. "FIFTEEN" – my alias – finally locked down, put to rest for the rumours of my death to circulate and be released into the atmosphere. Wow, from hustling on the block to being shot twice by the police and then sent to jail and taken care of like a sick, dying baby.

My first night I was scared. Why? Because we are human and when you're being carried down a dark, dirty corridor like this with a foot that is turning green and swelled up like a dead, decaying dog and smells just the same then you're supposed to be afraid.

When you feel the heat from all the bodies and hear the shouts from dorm to dorm and smell the pee and shit and perspiration and taste your own tears that disguise themselves in your sweat then you understand. You understand that there is no escape, either you cry in pain or your deal with it and I made up my mind on April the tenth 2008, that, so help me God, I was going to stop them in their tracks and say, "Hey Mister Officer, I is no punk so don't be stupid!"

I had another reason to be scared. In 2006 I came up in this crazy place – for resisting arrest, disturbing the peace, assault and obscene language – I was about 15 years old and still attending Point Fortin College. When I came up, I came up with all my burdens and 'bad boy' behaviour. I was a menace in those days, and I don't mean that in any boasting way. When I walked down the covered stretch I felt uncertainty.

You see, when you're taken and put in a place full of young people like yourself with the same mindset and hate inside of them, then you wouldn't know what to expect either.

That night I got beat up by 16 others but as I said, I'm not a punk so I did my best to throw back a few fists then I just rolled up in a corner, covered my head and blanked out my mind. I never begged or called for help. I took it. I took the 32 fists pounding aimlessly against my body, I took it, my God knows I took it. But, as I said before, the hate I had inside of me was shared by every single young man inside at that time.

The next night I gave some poor kid what I got, then every night after that I gave, and gave and gave some more. It felt good, but it was wrong. In 2008 when I 'returned' I expected another beating despite my injury. It was like, "O.K., guys, let's get it over with!" That didn't happen though. I was properly well taken care of. I was given all the needed jail stuff.

It really is funny though. One of my village mates KB was locked up for some house breaking gig. He and another East Indian kid held my swollen foot while being transported from Siparia Police Station – I attended Point Fortin Magistrate's court. We picked up the kid and his charge partners in Siparia – and headed for the Youth Training Centre where they made sure I was covered. I got a bed, sheet, toothbrush, towel and you know the needed stuff.

I was greeted with "What de Fuh.., Marky boy!!" I was too weak to answer but I smiled 'cause (sic) someone wasn't exactly 'happy' to see me but felt comforted by my arrival. Kon and I used to fight with each other any time we see each other, anywhere our eyes see was war. That was when we were about 12 or 13 years old. I was already doing crime and Kon was still getting permission to play outside, but the little bugger had heart and rage.

Writing this down and remembering it reminds me of Mikey Harrold Robbins' book Never Love a Stranger: *Kon was determined to fight and stand up for himself no matter how bad the scuffle. Eventually we put aside our differences, mainly because of his big brother, Saddam, who was also my "crime guardian" in a twisted, fruit punch kind of way.*

We both began smoking weed together and became very close friends. It was he who helped me out that cold, bitter first night. While I lay in pain he spoke to me about our homes and schools. It was cool despite my throbbing foot.

In those days we didn't have televisions, fans, computers, tables and chairs in every dormitory. The most that could be done is that one could stay in the back of the dormitory, watch the 4-foot fluorescent bulbs lined on the grey and red steel beam on the roof, lay down on one's bed and think and listen and wonder and get mad and pissed at being in a steamy room filled with stink smelling nobodies that consider themselves 'bad' cause they're in jail. Fools! It's not their fault, but if not whose fault is it?

I felt relieved when I finally lay back on the chewed up mattress and looked around. I saw smoke rising in the distance and a whiff of marijuana climbed up my nose and danced the salsa in my head, but I was in too much pain to smoke. I smiled, not at anything inside these walls, but at getting away…with life and a small gold ring with the initials MR written neatly across it, indented.

I was alive and when a Galil, semi-automatic is aiming at your back and you jump a wall – that seemed too high – and got hit in your foot causing a numbing pain and shocking feeling to overtake you or your arm is pushed violently forward from the bullet of a 9 mm pistol then, you could smile. You could feel proud to know that you survived – might be by the skin of your teeth – but you survived man!

*****

Time drags behind these multi-coloured walls that are decorated with gang names and "was here" messages. An hour feels like if it's been magnified. The nights – in 2008 and 2009 – were warm and sticky. It was enough to make your skin grow moss like an old rock that is constantly being soaked.

Laughter could be heard as young, criminal men boasted about their crimes: who they made scream and beg or how they came so very close to death, but escaped. Some of them would lie just to fit in and some would be so honest you think they're lying while in fact it's more real than the hairs on your head. Pictures of blood gushing and innocent people crying with their faces expressing nothing but hurt and a need for revenge are stamped in your mind. Yes, all of this was seen and heard and felt in one night, one night alone and despite the other lads around me that's how I felt: alone.

I was arrested and charged for a number of criminal offences – they (the police) tried pinning many more on me but they wouldn't stick – all of which I did alone. I got charged for:

Three counts of armed robbery: guilty

Possession of arms and ammunition: guilty

Assault: guilty

Rape: Not guilty – got that right. I don't deal in rape.

Kidnapping: guilty – That I deny too.

When I took out my charge papers and showed them to Kon a crowd gathered around us. I mean these kids were amazed. Not only was it a lot of charges but they weren't "petty" cases either. I had two capital charges: kidnapping and rape. And whether guilty or not guilty; I had a gang-green foot and a reputation to protect.

Part Two:

A relative had given the order, but come to think of it, he gave the orders right from the beginning. I admired this relative for many reasons, but mainly because he held down a family, had girls and still played a big part of the block. When I say that he had given the order I'm speaking about when he said not to give me the gun.

He didn't plead or beg "Moon Dog", "Gangster" or "Emi" not to give it to me, it was a simple, "Mertle wha' yuh feel?" asked by Gangster and then an even simpler, "Nah boy" said by my blood: Travis.

I felt a rage build inside of me, a kinda (sic) "do anything to anyone" rage. Some people might go on to say it was some demonic spirit deep inside of my guilt holding my will power and twisting it until it surrendered to internal bleeding and nothing more.

I wouldn't agree to that, I'd say that my willpower died a long, long time before that – some time in the early 2000s when Bin Laden was bombing up the place.

What hurt most of all was that the .44 Venezuelan special – rubber, hard plastic and steel – was mine not theirs. I didn't want to travel the distance I had to with it so I left it in my home town until I could get a driver. I didn't want to believe it and I refused to let it sink in.

I watched him, high and drunk at the same time, eight o'clock in the morning. I watched the four of them laugh in my stupid mind too, why? Because I knew that they couldn't stop anything even if they played with its wires and cut a few. My future had already been decided: it was already finalised in heaven, behind those marble gates.

On April 7th – a Monday – at about 9:15 I would be shot twice and on February 20, 2009 – a Friday – I would be sentenced to three, long, hard agonising years in YTC.

I had money, but greed is a funny thing. Even if we are afraid to admit our lust for money it's there. I wanted more than $1500 to go back home with. I wanted to be comfortable and $500 couldn't do it – not me, Friday: the young Don of Vance River needed more. He always needed more. Nothing was enough.

I never would have foreseen my pain if the three ghosts from A Christmas Carol had come and given me a visit.

It hurts though, remembering this, seeing Travis's face inside the courthouse, disappointed, hurt, angry at his young nephew, for disobeying his instructions and ending up in jail. Herbert Charles – the magistrate – read out my charges, "Marc Friday, you are charged for robbing…of this and that and the other, valued at this, that and the other."

He read that charge three times against three different people in the space of a week – Tuesday to Thursday. "Herbie" then went on to read a charge of kidnapping, rape and assault. It didn't feel good to be accused of rape not with my knowledge and experience with and of women. I'm no rapist, believe that!

I couldn't go to court for a couple of weeks because I was transported to the hospital the day after I landed in YTC. I spent those weeks handcuffed to a bed and my left foot in a cast – their idea not mine. I was being watched like some kind of criminal (Ha!) from the police. The warrant for me being kept in YTC had expired as well. I was charged for so many crimes. Even though I had better sense than to run, the police had to guard me. Those days of my prison term were days worth remembering especially Mrs John-Joseph who was the infirmary officer responsible for my being sent to Port-of-Spain General Hospital.

Please don't mind if I stray for a minute, but this woman is worth taking a minute for. She has dimples deep like the Atlantic Ocean. Her eyes are caramel brown with long, sexy eyelashes, round face, straight, jet black hair – at one time. Now there are brown, eye-catching streaks and fully dyed ends. She's a big-boned woman but her "swag" makes her a model, much better than those Somalian famine victims that Tyra Banks has on America's Top Model with ribs not worthy of a Thanksgiving.

Mrs Joe's skin is what we call "red". She really is a sweet Trini woman. I still see her checking my infected foot and covering her nose but yet still doing her job: she still washed my foot the best she could – despite the stench of my decaying foot.

I saw people leave the hospital and I saw some go in. I wasn't condemned because I was from YTC. I wasn't treated with any form of disrespect or scorn. I wasn't equal because, in a real sense, I was still from YTC. I interacted with some patients and that felt good.

Eventually I got a cell phone so I was able to call some of the people that I considered "close". Omella, one of my loves, kept me company. I told her once that I'm not coming out any time soon.

She didn't cry or have any movie type of reaction. She laughed a kind of "Hmph". My laugh was more noticeable. I asked her if she could stay without a man for three years. She said, "I'll try." I called from in my cell a couple of months after I got sentenced. (It is possible to get your hands on a cell phone in prison). She got a man, no biggie, though I was still glad to make her break his rules.

In YTC I could look back and remember seeing her on my last day home. We sat in the back of "Dog's" house and spoke about stuff for a while. She had a bag with bread, onions, eggs and other things for a nice, hearty breakfast. She had a black, plastic bag with legal stuff swimming in her hand. I had $300 worth of "jam, jam" weed in a small see-through plastic bag in mine.

The morning sun, the corn birds, the voices, the water springing from a broken WASA pipe in the middle of the road, the breeze, cool, gentle, calm. All of this made me smile when I saw her. The smell that the breeze brought was her perfume, the whistling of the corn birds and the sound of the voices complimenting her made me look up and thank God for life; the morning sun made her hair shine and her neat corn-rolled hair looked….

The broken pipe opened space for a good concentration to bubble in our sworn love: young, unknowledgeable love. I think that was the only time of the day that crime didn't run circles in my brain. She took my mind off the gambling and smoking that was taking place in Moon Dog's living room. When my phone rang and my right-hand man, Moon, told me the police were raiding one of our team member's block in Vessigney, Omella went to tell Man, another one of our "teammates" and I warned the guys inside the house.

I made myself invisible because – as funny as it may sound – I was trying to avoid jail time. (Hah!) It's ok if you laugh, I mean I ran from being on the block, but I later ran into handcuffs and a gang-green foot. But anyway, after running for what seemed like three zillion miles I called her. She laughed at how the police made us run like if we were one of those big eye greys on the Vance River Beach – they run into the water and she compared us to that!

Being in the crazy place and thinking about that day – and thinking mostly of one of my closest female companions – is enough to make tears crawl out onto this page and soak through this mattress making it too wet for me to sleep comfortable. It's not an easy thing to still have love for a girl after being away from her for three years and six months – that's how long I've been here. It's the 8th of October, 2011.

Part Three

My Regrets

"I don't regret shit!" Those are my words and I mean it. I don't regret being away from Omella or any of those girls that loved me or who I loved. I don't regret getting shot twice or spending three, long months in a hospital "dress". I don't regret making my mom cry neither do I regret the tears of my extended family shedding painful tears for weeks upon weeks.

If I regret any of it, then I regret being born into my village and family. I don't deny being "15" or "Marky" but I'd rather take that part of me and put in a glass wine bottle – a 1718 style of bottle and throw it into the Caribbean Sea.

I admit I'm sad because I caused myself pain, but I'm not ashamed of anything I did. I ask myself "What did these people expect?" I'm me. I'm not a fairy tale character, I'm a real life "ghetto" king. I am Marc Friday and I love myself. Yeah, I did things, but it was all on the path of being me.

I watch myself now and I feel so good it's a shame! How could I regret making the decisions I made? It gave me a path. When I stood in our bathroom – at home by my grandfather – I always found some kind of fault with my appearance. I believed that even if no one cared, looking good was first priority – at all times.

I miss a lot of simple stuff though. I miss the fresh ocean breeze that swept Vance River away. I miss being home and waiting for a certain time to go and conduct business. I miss sitting in the pavilion and playing all-fours and sharing one cigarette with three others. I miss being home, the scent is foreign to me now. I don't even know if my bedroom is still my bedroom.

Most of my clothes are, most likely, decaying in some dump in Point Fortin. I didn't have any radio or T.V. in my room 'cause I don't think I had time to sit and watch T.V. I really am wasting my time in this…place. Three years isn't that long but for a youngun like me to be in one spot, one place, under one roof for more than one year is amazing. I must say, for real, they've penned a lion amongst men, an eagle amongst kiskidees. "Forgive them Father they know not what they've done."

163

I have gained knowledge – a lot – that could either carry me in the right way or in the wrong way. I know about the wrong, but times have changed. Since 2008 we're in 2011 – at least I am. Who knows. You could be in the year 2034. And the things I've seen are fantastic: the technology, the halls built for cultural performances, the housed homeless, the dropping crime rate (isn't it dropping?) my baby brother.

Being up in this place gave me room – and time – to think and see and understand. How can I regret the things I've done? It was those things that put pictures in my head and a pen in my hand. Those cruel and wicked deeds of mine gave me a vision and that vision gave me hope and helped me to place myself in a circle that I could learn and teach and lead. My vision at first was to be a boss and let those stupid kids that figure they know life to sell weed and crack for me. I had my mind sent on one thing: letting people – innocent or guilty – feel my pain. But I'm moving on from that.

Times have changed since then. I still want that power, that invincible and invisible feeing that only a gun and a mask could make you feel. I still feel that hate inside of me. I mean I haven't seen any one of those old, rotten brain cracks from Vance River; I didn't have a lot of love in my heart for any of them anyway. I, the lone start that pops up early in the morning: I'm only nice when you see me and take a breath and notice. Other than that I'm like the plant you forget in your backyard.

I have a lot of lovely people praying and depending on me. I have got to make it but, in real, I am not suffering! I'm willing to work and make money and get married, have two kids, a house, car, 60" Internet TV, fish tank – with golden fish from Malaysia – and an indoor pompek named Peaches. I want to be a star if not for the world then at least for my family.

I feel to cry 'cause it's hard, but I guess I'd have to suck it up until my freedom date – a date that has, without a doubt, became the most important day for me right now. I don't know why I chose crime – I don't. A lot of folks say that I don't have a troublesome aura and I could be one of the best, but how I am is not how I really want to be.

I want to have everything in my reach. I would like for my family to be just that: a family not just people that carry the same surname and look alike in some ways. I would like to feel love – to give and receive – everyone but my heart isn't really a loving heart unless, well I choose to make it and believe you = me. That's hard. I want a bedroom not a "bed spot" or "cell". Is this how we're supposed to live: in fear of people like me or people like me behind some cold, rust-smelling, paint-fading bars?

At times I think I'm nothing but an ass with a fake vision and a bag of dreams on my back, who's buying? Crime and violence is real and I regret not saying no. Jail? It's inevitable for a person that chooses the broad road with big Vegas lights and strippers in every window like Christmas curtains on December 19. That's why I don't regret anything that I did; that's why I never liked big 30-year-old men flirting with girls my age. I'll be 30+ and I know I might do the same. But this is my time now. I'm not supposed to feel like that but c'mon there are a lot of freaks in the world and even if I might grow up to be king freak of them all I still am entitled to share my voice, my opinion.

My grandmother died while I was behind this stupid fence. She died without seeing hair on my face and the weight that I put on. She died without seeing my smile; my skin; my eyes; my…love. I wanted to cry, but no matter how much I tried they refused to make themselves present. Don't think I don't love her, that's out of the question. I had mad love for that brown skin, thick, paralysed woman. I loved her more than Santa Claus loves his prized reindeer and the little annoying elves that made a Batman figure for me in '96.

I could have spoken to her about anything – good, bad and twisted. She was my counselor. Not seeing her before she went home was like getting thrown into the Arctic Ocean with a black bag over my head. Losing her was like losing my only pair of shoes; you know, you'll search the same spot over and over and even though you know subconsciously they're gone, you refuse to believe that your last hope has vanished.

She wasn't a saint, and I know that on the day of judgment we'll meet and if she and my mom and my Aunt Valery would for some reason be slowly proceeding to hell then I would beg and beg and if my begging doesn't work then – my mind might change but right now it's from the heart – I'd go too just to be close to them. Is that love?

This was Marc: raw, uncensored and uncorrected. Profound, a bit flawed, his handwriting always surprised me. He took errors like "gang-green" and made them a style. He had learned the meaning of "sic" and put that in his writing. That was Marc.

My First Night in YTC – Jahmai

It was at this time I finally noticed the seriousness of my situation. The prison transport van came to a halt in front of the double chain linked gate. It opened. I was being escorted into YTC along with my two friends who were also charged with the same offenses as me. I arrived at dark, probably 7:30 p.m., only to find out from the officer who had opened the gate that we would be the last prisoners to come in for the night.

As we entered a little room furnished with one desk, there were two lazy-looking officers and a wire cage about 7' by 7'. Before we were ordered into the cage, we were ordered to strip all our clothes in the corridor that we had just entered. I will never forget that feeling. I stood in shock not moving an inch of my body complying with the instructions given. Not even at home can I ever remember taking off my clothes in front of anyone other than my girlfriend.

As I turned to my left, then right, my friends were already nude and being examined by the officers. With a few harsh words, obscenities, directed to me to hurry up and comply, I finally did, feeling most embarrassed. This might sound strange but all I could think of was how I would react if one of the officers or the prisoners I were about to meet were to approach me sexually. From this point on, this was my only thought.

After I was searched for contraband and nothing was found, I was allowed to dress again. This I did as fast as possible. I had nothing of my own except the clothes on my back and the shoes on my feet. After a briefing from the same two lazy-looking officers who didn't move a muscle when I was being searched I was told what my behaviour was supposed to be like. I was given a toothbrush, a blue soap – like the one my mother washes whites with – and toothpaste, and then directed out to where all the prisoners are housed.

At this pointed I wanted out of this place (YTC). I started hearing the prisoners before I could see them, and when I finally did, they all seemed like mini hulks to me since they were all twice or three times my size. The officer (a new officer) offered me dinner – in their terms "diet" but I refused because of the pack of flies that I saw sitting on the vessels containing the food. I cannot even remember if I was angry or not when I first came in. All I knew is that I was not going to eat that "sick" stuff they were offering.

Starting again to move along the corridor to my unknown location, my semi-fearful mood began changing into rage, silent rage because I was further into the reality of my irreversible situation. As I made my way up the corridor, I noticed some familiar faces, some strange ones, fearful looking ones and some that even looked like their owners were on the verge of death.

It was here when my charge partners and I decided what type of face we would portray while we were going to be housed here. We all agreed that we were going to be like ones that said if you messed with me, I'll go out of my way to be sure that I hurt you – most likely physically. Around that time in my life I thought that being aggressive was what earned you respect, love, money, happiness and enemies.

Now, after I'd decided how I wanted to be treated I was placed on my first test. I now began my journey along the remanded section where the boys are kept for crimes like murder. This section smelled worse than the convicted side. It was louder. The prisoners were issuing more threats and disrespectful remarks and they all looked more vicious.

I kept hearing them asking the officer who escorted us for him to put me in their cells. It was at this time that I knew I had nobody except my "chargy" (my partner charged with me) who would look out for my well-being because I knew nobody down here.

Before I was placed into a cell, the officer told me that if I were to run into a problem in the cell assigned to me that I should call for help. He said that these boys would want my gold teeth, my shoes, my clothes, just for either wanting them sake or to sell them for stuff to smoke.

When I heard what they would want my stuff for, calling for help would be the last thing on my mind. I thought to myself: I paid for my own trends – no mommy, no daddy – but me. I was going to fight to maintain my stuff just as I fought to obtain them. Now would be the time when all would be decided. It was either I was going to live up to the standard I'd set for myself or turn and be a coward now that we had been issued a cell.

Questions came raging in at us, "How much did your dental work cost? Where can I get that done? Are you selling those shoes? Clothes? Do you have anything to smoke?

This was just a pinch of the million questions asked. I noticed all but about five or six boys at the back of the cell that didn't move when my "charges" (other boys charged at the same time as me) and I entered. As I am good at assessing a situation I deemed them as what boys in YTC call "rankers".

They were dressed better than the rest of the fellows in the cell and had bigger and more prestigious spaces as well. Automatically I knew I wanted to be like them. After all the brief interviewing that rubbed my "charges" the wrong way was over I could identify who was willing to defend themselves, who wasn't, who were searching for leaders to guide them and who simply didn't exist.

Before I approached the esteemed "rankers", I took the end of my toothbrush and sharpened it to a point so it could be used as a weapon. I've heard a lot about jail before, about what stands and what should get you cut but here it seemed that nothing stood.

Everyone that hears about jail has a certain perception about it, but it is only when you arrive you experience, not just see, the hidden reality of a whole other world.

When I finally approached the "rankers" without hesitation they accepted me as an equal. I was awarded a clean bed, sheet and space, so too were my charges. The thought of deceit never crossed my mind. I came from one crime unit before jail and was now a part of another in jail. In all crime units loyalty is a recommended trait and clearly I wanted to prove myself worthy to my new clique.

After my mind was at a little more ease I could now start again to think of my family, friends and how I was going to get out of jail. I went into further concentration when the officer passed at nine o'clock and ordered everyone to sleep. Of course everyone was still sneaking around doing their own thing, but I needed the rest so I went to sleep with my toothbrush weapon in my waist because to some extent I was still a bit unsure of all the new company that surrounded me. That was my first night in YTC.

The Story of Ralph

I thought we'd all breathe a sigh of relief and live happily ever after once the weight of that CXC exam didn't loom over us again, but there is no perfect moment in time. Yes, we didn't need to worry about an exam any more. It was over and all out of our hands. We could relax and breathe a sigh of relief.

Mr Stewart and Ms McDonald said we could do anything we wanted after the exam. We could do fun things, a play perhaps, some creative writing. The idea was for me to stay with this group and see them through their sentences.

My boys knew this, but they decided to go straight into CXC English literature.

"I'm not going to leave you," I said. "I'm going to see you through this and Mr Stewart and Ms McDonald promised we could stay together no matter what. We don't have to do another course."

"No," they said. "We want to do something meaningful. Another CXC English class."

I might have been trying to talk them out of doing another course because I was upset. My first time back to YTC after the exam, I learned that in between the two parts of the CXC English Language exam, a guard had decided to confront Kheelon about a cell phone found in his dorm.

"This couldn't have waited until after the exam?" I asked Ms McDonald. She too was upset. I knew Kheelon didn't have a chance to pass the exam after that guard had jumbied him. Kheelon confirmed my suspicions: he couldn't focus on the second half of the exam.

Along with this bad news came a surprise: a new student for CXC English literature. I'll call him Ralph because his case still has not reached court. Ralph, like so many boys in remand in YTC, had spent years waiting for his murder case to work its way up to High Court. He had been in YTC for over five years.

A quiet young man filled with sorrow and grief, Ralph slipped into class one day and sat in the front row. He smiled, mimed "Hi" so that I would notice him, and then slipped to the back of the class for most of the subsequent classes. He wrote about himself in third person like the South African writer J.M. Coetzee had done in his autobiography, *Boyhood*.

In Ralph's story he spoke of the "grief of losing the one symbol of hope in his life: Grief over losing the one thing life gave him to hold and cherish: a mother; grief of losing the one person who believed in him, a mother; grief of losing his adopted mother at 14, grief of losing his one, true mother at childbirth and losing the other to sickness."

When Ralph learned that he was adopted, he descended into a dark world of drugs, alcohol and anger that led him to be charged with an unthinkable crime: murder.

Ralph rarely spoke, but he enjoyed writing. He too wrote about his first night in YTC:

> *Carefully examining my new home, I realised this cell was built for one prisoner. The walls were dirty with what appeared to be faeces wiped on the surface, a replacement for toilet paper. It was everywhere, dried and hard, almost like a wall painting.*
>
> *In one corner a six-feet long iron bed was placed in the overcrowded the cell as it took away half of the moving space. The other side was occupied by a toilet, a sink and two small shelves.*
>
> *All of this made the cell smelly with urine or faeces, stuffy and stifling. One section of the wall, one pair of ventilation vents 15 cm in width and six inches long, meant not much breeze came through there. It*

was used to dry wet clothes. I had no place to rest my head for the night except under the iron bed frame, which was dark, dusty, a place where mosquitoes and cockroaches roamed.

One of the boys stood in a corner with a menacing look. No warm welcome, sympathy or cheer was in this atmosphere. The lads in the cell were really angry like lions that defend their territory when invaded. Luckily, the officer standing watch outside understood this, and I knew if I were left alone behind a closed gate with these vicious animals it would be my last night. From that point, I knew they were masters who would eat me up and spit me out dry like in the movies. I was taken to another cell.

The only difference here was that lads kept their room and space filled with their status: toiletries and canteen snacks. Cobwebs hung like Christmas lights strung across the ceiling. I had entered a world that I didn't even know existed.

Ralph had a different story of survival in YTC. He wrote:

Once upon a fraction of my life in prison something shaped my being in a bittersweet way. Put simply, other people's perception of me began to define who I am – not the other way around. What people say and think about you will eventually control how they react with you. These became the foundation blocks of my picture perfect world.

I would describe myself as withdrawn and bitter. People had a different picture of me. One day, a lad said I was mad and from that day, this description was added to my character whether I liked it or not. It started when I first reached YTC. Everyone thought I looked real mad.

Then, when they discovered the crime I committed, that reinforced their beliefs a little. When the court sent me to St Ann's Mental Complex, without a doubt, they deemed me mad, and so it began.

At first, this was new to me because no one had ever called me that before. It never occurred to me when I was living in freedom without the bars. Then I just grew into it once I was behind bars. I started believing it, and eventually behaving as such, not only because that's what the world around me expects, but also this expectation gave me a door of opportunity.

Seeing everyone believes I'm one of those lads who is "crazy" not just anyone would violate me. This was a real plus. No one ever lashed me. They just pick on me with cruel words and gestures. They themselves created a monster, and protected it just as much. So it was quite convenient knowing I was a coward and couldn't fight if my life depended on it.

I remember one time in the dorm everyone who was up prowling at night and playing tricks on people sleeping, stopped when it was time to play the pranks on me. Someone shouted, "No not that one. He real mad," and no one played with me, then till now.

It is said that quiet people are the ones to watch and since I was natural at being quiet and also deemed mad, well, it all worked together real well for me.

I now realise that it is mostly my quietness that connects me to their beliefs of me being mad. So this was my defense mechanism. The only way this image was ever dented is whenever I opened up myself.

You see, many people tried their utmost to encourage me to open up and relate to others. So when I took up their advice and opened up I did feel free inside, but empty at the same time. What made matters worse is that whenever I opened up myself to others those that were once afraid of me, and deemed me mad, no longer were afraid.

They began to see me differently for who I really was and not who they perceived me as. So as a result the respect and false impression of fear was gone and out came more cruel words and abuse – not hitting but walking all over you kind of things: abuse.

I started to dislike myself for the betrayal of my own tongue against me, that one thing that defines who I am in front of others. Now that my character has changed from quiet to more socially active and involved, my body helplessly and voluntarily speaks out, revealing itself, reaching out to others, and at the same time developing myself yet cursing it as well.

The more they see and hear of me the more disrespectful and rude they get, making me regret what I started: talking. The bitter sweet. The perfect picture. The rise and fall of myself.

Madness is not remaining quiet. It is speaking out and being hated for it. You're quiet, they deem you mad, but some want you to talk. You talk, they deem you foolish, normal and cowardly, but some are glad for your openness. Then, caught in the middle you're helpless and not really pleasing yourself. The tongue is to blame for this perfect picture. That part of me, my tongue, defines who I am.

Like my other students, Ralph's assessment included the paragraph about what animal you would choose to be. He wrote:

I would have to choose among a bird, a dog and an ant. A bird because flying through the sky thousands of miles alone, far from earth sounds exciting; a dog because it's said to be man's best friend. Sometimes humans treat their dogs with more care than their own families, and lastly an ant because it's always good to have a brother backing you up strong. Since they move in groups of thousands, they're an army.

These animals symbolise who I am. Sometimes I prefer to be alone like a bird in the sky or feel loved by my master like a dog. But as humans we don't do much of watching over each other like that. I would rather be an ant so that I could enjoy something I don't have around me: togetherness.

Ralph wrote an entire notebook of essays about *The Wine of Astonishment* by Earl Lovelace.

Sometimes, like a mirror, I see my reflection looking back at me through pages behind a hard cover. I was once told that through reading a book the journey of life becomes much easier because you establish who you really are after each page turned or your see different aspects of yourself.

Reading Wine of Astonishment *painted portraits that represented symbolic and realistic scenes of my life. One such scene is in the beginning and sadly the ending of* Wine of Astonishment.

The summary of events can be broken down simply like this: The church was hopeful and strong at one point in time, but challenged when faced with the added stress brought by the Government, law, other churches and their own selves.

They were all piled on top of each other like lava trying to burst from a volcano. So is my life, suffocating in the rubble of disappointment and failures, rejection, shame, ridicule, insults and oppression. In the darkness, each door that leads into light is entered and suddenly vanishes like vapour. Hold on to the rope and it snaps. Yet they say fight. So I fight, fall, fight, crawl, fight, scream, fight, bleed, fight, give up and try, but fail until maybe the day I'm set free.

The irony is, all this struggling has worn me down and if I am set free, just like the church in Wine of Astonishment, *my spirit would die leaving only a shell – like the church – the wind could easily blow by without saying goodbye.*

In his essays, Ralph played with structure, and he analysed information with great care and insight. I didn't know how to respond to Ralph's pain so as usual, I wrote a letter.

Dear Ralph,

I do not wish to preach or cross any boundaries that you have established, and I don't want to make you feel uncomfortable in any way by begging to differ with any of the observations you have about yourself, but I really believe this: You and Marc have the potential to be two of the best writers to ever come out of the Caribbean. You are capable of being world-class writers who will make Trinidad proud. Your insights and experiences – difficult and painful as they have been – make you a finely nuanced writer.

You pack so much information and feelings into a sentence. You develop your thoughts In totally unexpected ways. You are a master of structure, and you create a framework that is truly a piece of art. Your writing feels like thousands of fine threads that you rescue from becoming tangled and then delicately weave together into a fine tapestry.

If you honour your writing, it will help you to discover yourself, understand yourself and accept yourself. It will become a vehicle for reclaiming yourself.

Don't give up on happiness. It comes in small measures. Even if it is fleeting, it is there and sometimes we can hang onto those special moments a little bit longer. I'm not giving up on you because I have caught too many glimpses of a remarkable young man with many creative gifts. There is a lot more there than you know; a lot more than you ever dreamed possible.

Sincerely,
Miss

Ralph's depression and his inability to forgive himself for the crime he committed weighed heavily on him at all times. He lived in perpetual darkness. A month before the CXC literature exam, Ralph felt so depressed he was put on medication that seriously impeded his ability to think, recall or sequence information.

All that work, I thought, and he might not pass because Ralph kept saying he couldn't concentrate. In my mind, he seemed to be a clear "1" so I was quite upset. But he did pass his CXC English literature exam with a "3". It turned out to be his only CXC pass that year, but Ralph already had five passes.

Letters to Shawn

Shawn had disappeared from class just before CXC English language exams. I understood why he did not come to class, but we missed him and wanted him to be a part of our English literature class. That could not happen because of Shawn's release date. I sent a letter to him through Jahmai.

Dear Shawn,

I miss having you in class. I understand the decision you have made to stay away from class just before exams, and I am so sorry that I did not find a way to make sure your name was on that list YTC had to turn in for the CXC English language exam. I did ask several times to make sure you were on the list, and I was told that you were. Still, that is not good enough. I should have found a way to see that list. The only disappointment I had in the results was not hearing about the "1" that you so rightfully deserved.

Your presence in class meant the world to me. It is unfair and unreasonable for adults to expect young people to help them or guide them in any way. Adults are supposed to do that for young people and yet you were my rock on so many occasions.

You seemed to have had an uncanny way of reading me and understanding my lack of confidence, and your encouraging notes kept me going in my darkest moments.

I know that it is in no way fair for your English class to boil down to what I learned because of you, but I learned a lot about myself as a person and a teacher.

God bless you. I thank him every day of my life for sending you to me.

Sincerely,
Miss

Dear Miss Jacob,

I know to start with this letter and my handwriting look strange to you, which is so wrong. The only reason I wasn't doing any work, Miss, is because I was feeling left out and odd. You know, Miss, like everyone was anticipating doing their exams and everything and Shawn wouldn't even be here. Anyway, Ms Jacob, I'm really going to try to do my English exam and some others first opportunity I get when I am out of here.

Since Sunday will be my last class with you in YTC this is more or less a letter of thanks to you. Thank you for everything, Miss. I really appreciated everything including the musical and the Christmas show you took us to. I'm sorry the whole class couldn't be there because some were in lockdown. I loved those shows. Coming from where I'm coming from that was some real high-class stuff for people like us, especially me, who are very sensitive. But don't tell anyone because I'm supposed to be a tough one in here.

Usually, Miss, whenever there is something going down I always ask to stay inside because I hate the fact that whenever we go on outings we are always "the boys from YTC" but when we went with you, we were "the boys from Ms Jacob's English class". That was the best label I ever wore.

When I get out I'm really interested in going to those kinds of things you know, be a "normal person" for once a "big boy" a "rich kid".

Right now I couldn't be happier I'm like going home on Thursday H-O-M-E.

No more of this sorry place. I met you and a lot of other important people but this is no place to like or even get comfortable in so I'm happy to be leaving. I'm not Government property anymore.

When I'm out, Ms Jacob I'll call you every so often. I hope in your busy schedule you can make time to call me too. I will never forget you. I mean like never. Whenever my mind runs on you I'll dial your number and I'll be seeing you as well. Remember you said, "You'll say that but no one has time for an old, white lady."

I'm determined to prove everyone wrong.

Maybe in the past, a long time ago, I was a criminal but not anymore. I'm just a usual individual right now. I'm going to behave myself and go to plays and learn my work. A tiny, little feeling inside of me says I'm more intelligent than I may think so I'm going to utilise that. I'm going home Thursday!!!

Thank you for all the food, generosity, humour and love you showed me over the 14 months I've known you.

Thank you, Miss Jacob
Shawn

When I finished reading Shawn's letter all the joy, sadness and fear of my first student going home hit me hard. I am guilty of relying on his strength and support inside YTC. I am determined that joy will prevail.

181

Dear Shawn,

These days, I am haunted by a famous short story called "A Very Old Man with Enormous Wings" by Colombian Nobel Laureate Gabriel Garcia Marquez. In this brilliant piece of magical realism, the scruffy, old man – with dirty white wings – lands in a village where he is first scorned by the villagers, and then put on display. One day, the old man musters the energy to fly away, leaving the villagers to wonder who or what the man really was. He could have been an angel who fell from grace they decided.

Maybe I can't get this story out of my mind because Marc wrote something last week about a guy who admires butterflies and dragonflies even though he knows that little boys rip their wings off.

Maybe I remember this story because last week while I was waiting for the guard to bring you all to class, I noticed a lad nearby with a set of bird feathers. He arranged them in his hand like he was organising a hand of cards or spreading out a delicate fan. He kept saying, "Pretty, so pretty. Aren't they pretty?"

All the lads who, were waiting with him for someone who comes to read books to them once a month, appeared to be mesmerised by the feathers. They nodded their heads, as though they were hypnotised, every time he said, "pretty."

On the first day of class you chose your own set of wings. You wrote, "I would like to be an eagle because of its ability to fly, and also because eagles always do the hunting. Eagles are never anyone's prey."

You and I both know this is not some sappy letter about angels. This is about wings. In the end, it doesn't matter if the very old man with enormous wings ever was an angel. What matters is that in the depth of despair, the old man with wings found a way to move on with his life – and he did it in a most spectacular way.

You are bright. You have a plan. You are going to finish your education. You will succeed in life, Shawn. I bet my wings on that.

Sincerely,
Miss

The Story of Vaughn

My students never asked me for anything. Still, I had taken for granted that giving was my job. I gave time, advice, books. Giving always came easier for me than receiving so I didn't think twice about refusing the gifts they offered me: biscuits they won in competitions like aerobics burnout; apples they received from relatives' visits. Then, one day, when Ashton offered me an apple yet again, it hit me: They wanted that same feeling I got from giving. They were learning to give, and all the joys that went with it, and I needed to feel comfortable receiving gifts.

There was always some unexpected lesson to learn in YTC. A simple exercise could bring great insights and shocking revelations about their thoughts or their past lives. I thought I had developed a good understanding of the type of teenager and young man who was in YTC. There were many inmates for violent armed robbery – robbery with a gun. There were many boys in remand for murder. Abuse, gangs, "wrong company" had shaped many of these angry lads' lives.

I didn't romanticise or justify their behaviour, their lives or their sentences. Neither did I scorn or judge them. That wasn't my job. My job was to teach them, and I had reached a relatively comfortable place in my mind because I knew basically what I was dealing with – or so I thought until the night that I brought some articles to class by the late *Express* journalist Keith Smith.

I took news stories, features, commentaries, and old stories by Keith from the *Express* archives. It was my way of paying tribute to Keith and making sure a new generation of newspaper readers knew of the invaluable contributions he had made to Caribbean journalism. Of course his work was an invaluable lesson in writing style and tone particularly with the use of Creole.

After that class, Vaughn approached me, and said, "Miss, so it is possible to get old stories off of the Internet – like from years ago?"

I said, "Yes."

Vaughn slipped me a folded sheet of paper.

"Could you see if you could find out anything about this person?" he said.

I read the name and agreed to find out information.

When I plugged the name on the Internet, I found commentaries about the death of the person Vaughn wanted information about. The man, a simple peanut vendor, had been killed while in police custody.

I pulled up transcripts of a High Court case that had been postponed for over ten years. Finally, the High Court said the case would be heard. No more delays by the police. The police decided to settle the case. The High Court delivered a blistering statement saying that this was one of the greatest travesties of justice it had ever seen. In the transcript there was mention of a child, a baby. I finally put two and two together: this was the story of Vaughn's father.

I thought, no wonder everything had turned out like it had for Vaughn who is in remand for murder. I didn't know what to do. How could I show him this scathing court report and these articles? I asked Mr Moore, the guidance counselor at school, and Ms McDonald what I should do and they both said, "You have to show him. Talk to him about it."

The next class, I gave Vaughn the papers to read. After class, I said, "We'll talk about this next week."

For the whole week I studied what to say, and couldn't come up with anything that seemed meaningful enough to me. On Saturday night, I pulled Vaughn aside to speak to him. "I'm so sorry about your dad. That should never have happened."

Vaughn looked shocked.

"You studying that Miss? Don't study that," Vaughn said. "My father was bound to die somehow. My father was a real bad man. He was in with Dole Chadee (a nefarious drug dealer in Trinidad who was eventually convicted and put to death by Government). Do you know how hard it was for me growing up, Miss? My mother tried to keep us all out of crime.

"She encouraged us to go to school, and we did. I played football. From the time I can remember, men in the neighbourhood used to push a gun in my hand and say, 'Here. Hold this. You have to live up to the reputation of your father, you know.'

"That's what I was facing. But I kept playing football. One day, we were at a football match at school, and someone said, 'There's a guy who just ransacked the locker rooms. He took all your stuff.'

"He took cell phones, shoes…. We knew who the person was so we reported it to the school and the police. They did nothing.

"At a next game, someone said the guy who stole our stuff was there and a fight was going on between him and a gang member who knew what he had done to us. The next thing we knew, the thief was dead. Stabbed once. I didn't even see his face."

Vaughn and some other boys present were arrested for the murder too. It was one of those cases where the police round up everyone in sight. Vaughn spent two years in YTC waiting for his trial even though the young man who did the stabbing had confessed and was quickly convicted of the crime.

When Vaughn finally went to court with three other boys from YTC, their cases were thrown out.

That is how I learned that there are many innocent boys in YTC as well. I didn't get a chance to say goodbye to Vaughn. I knew he was going to court, but usually the boys went to court and came right back to YTC because their cases had been postponed. I knew cases were postponed for years.

But I did get a chance to write a letter to Vaughn.

Dear Vaughn,

Although I knew this day was coming, I still felt surprised – not to mention happy – at the news last week that the San Fernando Magistrates Court set you free. Your story haunts me and makes me question our justice system.

Looking back over the time we spent together in my CXC English language class, I recall how you transformed from a quiet, guarded teenager to an outspoken, open, smiling young man. On the first day of class, you wrote very little about yourself, but I soon realised that you possessed an amazing amount of perseverance.

You were among the final group because you came to class religiously. We both knew that you would not be taking the CXC English exam, but that didn't matter to you. You just wanted to be in that English class.

"English was one of my favourite subjects in school," you wrote, "and I didn't get to do it because I was locked up." The circumstances surrounding the day that you were arrested would have made most people angry and bitter, but you have a penchant for transcending negativity, and you always make the most of your situation. Inside YTC, you played football and pan. You participated in every programme you could, and you never gave up coming to English class. You were a diligent student who grew confident and expressive. I admired your commitment to everything you tackled.

For me, one of your biggest accomplishments was that you learned to love reading. V.S. Naipaul's *Miguel Street* and Kalisha Buckhannon's *Upstate*, were two of your favourite books.

One class when everyone wrote descriptive essays, you showed me an essay you wrote about me saying how I was more than a teacher. "You are always caring. You are like a mother to us," you wrote, "and we appreciate that." You spoke about your own mother with the utmost respect, and nothing seemed to excite you more than a visit from her.

"My mother always instilled values in us: Do good. Go to school. Work hard," you told me.

Last night, I came across a letter I wrote to my English class after I finished reading *A Big Little Life: A Memoir of a Joyful Dog, Trixie* by Dean Koontz.

The author writes about how complex the world is. He says the only way to measure our lives is the way that we influence people.

As you re-enter the real world, I hope you will remember that letter. Be kind. Be good. Continue your studies and don't stop playing football. Search for your purpose in life. Surround yourself with true friends – honest young men who work hard to achieve their goals. A friend can only be a person who will add something positive to your life. Never allow anyone or anything to disillusion you.

When times get tough, remember you have always been a survivor. More importantly, when times were tough, you found a way to move forward in your life. I know that those lessons from *A Big Little*

Life came to my mind when I decided to write this letter to you because when I asked which animal you would choose to be in life on that first day, you wrote, "I would choose to be a dog because of its freedom."

You are free now. Make the most of your life. I have seen you demonstrate amazing compassion to the remandees who had just entered YTC. Find someone to give hope to you in your community like you used to help the new lads, especially the very young ones, who came to YTC.

I will miss you in class, Vaughn. I know I will keep looking at that empty chair in our classroom and imagine when you sat there, but I am happy that you are beginning this new chapter in your life.

Sincerely,
Miss

The Results Are In

*I had grown to feel more confident about the direction
I had taken – namely discarding the textbooks for the
most part and using my own material to teach for the
exam.*

I knew my students had been in the best shape possible
considering our time restraints. I didn't want anyone
to become disappointed with his results so I had said,
"Remember, we're trying something here. Promise me, no
matter what happens, we're not going to give up."

"We promise," they had said.

Kheelon felt he needed more time to prepare for
the exam. I knew that he had moved up enough to get a
"4." I was hoping for a "3" and if he couldn't get that, I had
hoped a "4" would inspire him to continue. He did not have
a chance on the exam because of the cell phone incident.
Kheelon would get a "5".

On the day of the exam, I could only think about how
far they had all come. They had transformed from distant,
guarded, reticent students into avid readers, eager learners
and compelling writers.

What's more important, they had become caring,
trusting, confident, articulate young men. In the end, here
is what happened: Shawn, the student I was most sure of
passing with flying colours because of his ability to plug
into a structure and write cookie-cutter essays, would have
been a definite "1." I would have bet my life on that.

My disappointment would have been mitigated had I
known that Shawn would get out of YTC the Christmas after

the exam and return in January to sit the exam inside of YTC as a free young man. Shawn got a "2" on that exam.

Ashton was one of my best students. I knew from the letters he wrote to me and the chapters he wrote for his own book that he would pass the exam if he could overcome his fear of writing an essay. Ashton must have done quite well because he received a "4" on the exam even though he was unable to finish two essays. That "4" boosted his confidence and made Ashton work harder. He came back to class, knocked off essays in a timely manner, and looked forward to taking the exam in January, 2012 with Shawn. Ashton had finally conquered his fear of writing an essay.

Unfortunately, the second time Ashton signed up for the exam he had to go to court on the same day.

I am sure Ashton would have received a "2." Neither of these experiences proved daunting for Ashton. He is still pursuing his studies.

Olton, my organised, optimistic, national rugby player who wanted to be a turtle got a "3" on his English exam. He is the epitome of diligence and perseverance, and I couldn't have been prouder of his pass.

Miguel, the young man from Maximum Security Prison who came to me four months before the exam; the young man Mr Stewart asked me to help because he had four good CXC passes but had not got through with his English language exam in two tries, received a "2" on the English language exam.

Marc, the creative writer, had been a big worry for me because he avoided writing summaries. I thought he needed more practice. Marc came through with a "2."

Peter my bright student who needed to move to learn, got a "2." I still remember his smile when I told him the results. "I'll take that," said Peter. He has grown – both academically and personally – by leaps and bounds, and I have enjoyed witnessing his transformation.

Then there was Jahmai, the young man who spent nearly two years in lockdown; the young man I had taught in lockdown for two months. Jahmai received a "1."

There were reasons to celebrate, but what my students said to me after the exam meant more to me than any exam results. It is impossible to convey how proud I am of all of them. I wrote notes to each student.

Dear Ashton,

In a place that is very dark and dismal you always prove that there is light even in the darkest places. Your smile and your positive attitude towards the Four you earned on your CXC English language exam was really the highlight of my English class yesterday.

You came very far to get that Four and I know from the bottom of my heart that if you practise more, you will get at least a Two.

Strength comes from perseverance. Don't give up. Keep trying.

In a place where it is basically every man for himself, you always show support and kindness. You demonstrate what it is to be a truly good person. You are a role model and you make me very proud to be your teacher.

Sincerely,
Miss

Dear Marc,

I am so proud of your Two in CXC, and I hope that you are proud of your accomplishments too. I am glad that you are still in my class. I know it will be a real challenge since you are working outside of YTC, but Jahmai will help you.

Sincerely,
Miss

Dear Jahmai,

You are my one and only "One"! I am so proud of you. You have come so far. You are a bright, impressive young man. I am on top of the world.

Sincerely,
Miss

Dear Miss,

Now I can comfortably exhale, Miss Jacob. CXC results are out and I got my one. You were right when you told me I had panicked for nothing and I probably did better than I thought. I really appreciate those extra life lessons you were able to teach us and I believe those lessons helped a lot, they truly encouraged us to stay focused and believe in ourselves.

Thank you for the time you invest in us, Miss. Without your style and sensible approach, this for me might not have been possible. Being comfortable around you caused me to value education on a whole new level and to also value another teacher's input where learning is concerned. This feeling that you provoked was so effective that I was able to pass my other endeavours during the same season.

Again, Miss, thank you very much. I hope and pray only for the best things to be granted to you in the future.

Thank you,
Jahmai

Decisions

My students knew about my columns in the Guardian *that chronicled our academic journey, and of course they gave me their blessings and encouraged me to go ahead with this book.*

A journalist must feel free to write whatever she needs to write, but I did not go into this venture as a journalist. I was a teacher and there are boundaries that come with that discipline. This has been a delicate balancing act between being a journalist and being a teacher.

After 16 months of careful consideration I decided to write about my students because I wanted everyone to meet the most amazing group of young men I have ever known. Their diligence, focus, trust and intelligence blew me away. Their willingness to face their problems and their anger impressed me. Their inability to take anything in life for granted – including love and support – moved me to tears.

Yes, I agonised over the decision about whether or not to write about my students, but in the end I felt that it was an extraordinary opportunity for people to get to know young men who represent a side of Trinidad and Tobago – and probably any country in that Caribbean – that most people have come to fear.

This was an opportunity to face some of the challenges of our educational system and to see how at-risk teenage boys approach learning.

I always had my students' privacy in mind, and I couldn't help but feel protective. I never wanted my students to feel exploited. At the same time, I knew that I would never be able to do full justice to the experience that we all shared.

There is a bond that develops between students and teachers that facilitates learning. This was a bond that we all had to work hard at. We had to suspend many prejudices; we had to develop a sense of trust.

For my students to believe in my direction and follow me through all my academic experiments still means the world to me. They gave me confidence like I have never experienced in my life.

My students always knew the assignments that I would feature in the columns that I wrote in the *Guardian*. I had saved much of their work – as I have always done with all my students – because I like to chart students' progress.

I asked permission to use their work, and even took copies sometimes to remind them exactly what was in the assignment in case they had forgotten. I remember saying, "You have to tell me what the boundaries will be for writing about you. There is no one thing that I have to write about. Anything can be left out if it makes you feel bad or uncomfortable."

 I chose – without consulting my students – to use all of their work with its final revisions. For the most part, I did not use the spelling errors or grammatical errors along the way or even their Creole because I wanted to demonstrate how well they could write. I did not want to expose all of their mistakes. Life had done enough of that for them already. I wanted to show the final stage of their writing.

This is not to say their essays are perfect. I have kept some of the imperfections especially if they reflect their own sense of expression like Marc writing "gang green" instead of gangrene.

As I had told Ashton, where my students came from and where they stood when I met them was never important to me. My concern had to be where they were heading in life.

I wanted to convey how close they got to perfection and record what level they had achieved while demonstrating there is always room for improvement.

During those many weeks that we spoke about the possibility of writing about them, my students made only one request: "You can write whatever you want, Miss. The only thing we ask is that you don't write anything to make people pity us," said Jahmai.

"We don't want pity. We can handle anything: disappointment or even hate – but not pity." All my students agreed with Jahmai. That was their only stipulation, and it remained their only request. They never asked me to censor anything I wrote.

This is the group of young men I taught: Jahmai, Marc, Shawn, Kheelon, Vaughn, Ashton, Peter, Miguel, Olton and finally Ralph, who later fell in for CXC English literature.

They have never blamed anyone for their lives or their circumstances. They have always taken full responsibility for their actions.

I wanted so much more than passes on the CXC English language exam for them. I wanted them to experience true learning. I wanted them to know themselves better. "English," I told them, "is about learning how to express yourself."

"English," they told me, "was about life."

It wasn't just something in a book. English taught them how to think and feel and express themselves like never before. It taught them to face the pain they felt and express the pain they had caused others.

I wanted my students to be able to think about their decisions in life, and grow into young men who will contribute to Trinidad and Tobago. I hope they will all go on to be productive citizens, and I know some of them will always be in my life.

There are still many things that give me a heavy heart. I am deeply disturbed by the amount of time that it takes for a case to work its way through the courts. All court cases in Trinidad and Tobago are postponed too many times. Often the police are not ready for a case when it reaches court. Sometimes they misplace or lose evidence. Often the police just don't bother to come to court.

Years go by with these young men sitting in YTC waiting for their cases to be heard. During my time teaching in YTC it was not unheard of to see young men 25 years old waiting for their case to be called. Some of those young men inside YTC, I have learned, are innocent and the justice system is robbing them of their youth. This is not justice.

Taking One Day at a Time

I have learned to take one day at a time. I often wonder if I made the right choices when I singled out certain boys for my class, and I try not to blame myself for not fighting harder to keep promising students who fell by the wayside before the final cut for that CXC English class. Is there something more I could have done? I try not to blame myself when I open up the newspaper and read bad news.

While most of Trinidad and Tobago celebrated Carnival 2013 and Super Blue's resurrection in Soca music with "Fantastic Friday", the newspapers carried grim stories of crime spiralling out of control.

In one story, a young man appeared as little more than a gruesome statistic with his name buried deep inside the opening paragraph of a crime story published by the *Trinidad Guardian*: "The murder toll climbed to 39 yesterday after a 22-year-old man was killed in a gang-related shooting in Laventille. According to reports, around 1:45 p.m. residents of Dan Kelly Village, Laventille, reported hearing gunshots. They checked and found Dorian "Tiger" Weekes, of Nelson Street, Port-of-Spain, lying between two houses."

This is the grim reality of a gang member slaughtered on his way to commit a crime in an ironic attempt to prevent a crime: his own death.

Newspaper reports said, "Police described Dorian as 'a well-known gunman.'"

That is true, but in the picture of Dorian Weekes there are some shades of grey. Dorian was one of my former students, one of the original 27 young men who came to my CXC English Language class in YTC, but vanished before the final cut. He did not stay long enough to form any real bond with me, but I knew Dorian well enough to know that he caught fleeting glimpses of a better life.

Dorian had "frenemies", but he also had real friends who cared and hoped he would go on the right path and make it in life.

Jahmai says, "The same way Dorian died was the same way he said he didn't want to die: lying on the road with a set of TV cameras on him. He also said that he would chill out on the wrongdoing and I think he really did in the beginning, probably up until he fell back under the same peer pressure that got him arrested."

None of Dorian's real friends make excuses for the hurt and pain he caused people through his life of crime. No one strives to glorify Dorian's choices. It's just helpful to understand Dorian's brief life.

"I know personally that he died as a result of his own wrongdoing because he was in trouble with the same people that got him in the end. Why was he there then? He was going to try and get one of them before they got him," said one of Dorian's friends.

Police reports said Dorian was wanted for a number of recent shootings in the area. Police speculated Dorian had been "walking along the road to meet a 'friend' who lived nearby when he was lured into the yard by his attackers. The occupants of the two houses where Weekes was found told police they did not see the gunmen because they were too frightened to look outside after hearing the gunshots."

In Trinidad and Tobago, no one ever sees anything when a crime takes place. This is a country of see no evil, hear no evil. Everyone is afraid to see or hear anything because they perceive that they will become victims. Few people trust the police; even fewer believe the police will or can protect them.

Dorian didn't want to be a target or a victim. He had made himself hard like steel a few years ago after he lost his father. After doing five years in prison for his crimes, Dorian's father came back home determined to make a new life. He got himself a job delivering chicken. One night, after his last run, he was gunned down.

That's when Dorian's life fell apart and he became bent on revenge.

"I remember Dorian didn't shed a tear at his father's funeral," said social worker and prisons welfare officer Roderick Beaumont. "Dorian made himself hard. He did his three years in YTC, but I thought Dorian would make it when he came out. He was such a boy."

Dorian went to live with his aunt when he came out of YTC.

Dorian's friends – the ones who were cheering him on to go straight – want you to know this: "Tell the young people that might read your columns not to give up when they run into financial shortcomings. Don't go off trying to take no job to shoot at anyone. That's for real, and I say this not because we're scared but because we always lose more than we gain. We upset the way that life is supposed to be."

Those friends leave this message: "Ghetto youths, one more day of being broke won't kill us, so we could afford to at least wait to see or even create a way to turn our situation back around."

Peter, my only student left in YTC from Dorian's class, asked me on my first visit after the news story if I remembered Dorian.

"He used to sit right there," he said pointing to an empty seat in the first row. He produced a picture of a bespectacled, smiling Dorian between two other boys participating in YTC's Sports' Day. Dorian looks like any quiet, reserved boy you would find in any school in Trinidad and Tobago.

On the first day of class Dorian wrote this for me:

If I were an animal, I would like to be a tiger. I like the way the animal survives in the forests. The tiger is a special animal because it's at the top of the food chain in its part of the world.

My favourite colour is orange. I love football and basketball. I am a very sensitive and joyous person all the time.

He expressed no anger or bitterness as many of the boys in the class did when they first opened up, and he dreamed sometimes of making it in life through sports. His heart and his mind told him an education was important enough to be one of the 27 volunteers to show up for class. Dorian didn't stay, but he returned to class occasionally. I never turned him away even though I knew he wasn't ready to sit the CXC English language exam because I couldn't forget what he wrote on that first evening of class:

The reason I want to be in this class is because education is a must in the world. If you don't have an education, you might become a nuisance in society. I really wanted to be enrolled in the class to get out of poverty and crime.

Dorian was just another young man who wanted a chance in life.

Looking Back

Dorian's story made me think back to the beginning of our classes, and I wondered now what my students thought as they reflected on the whole experience. We had built a strong enough relationship that I felt I could ask them questions about our class.

"What was the biggest surprise on the first day of class?" I asked Olton, Kheelon, Jahmai, Marc and Peter. Without knowing what the other had answered, they all came up with the same response: "You didn't come with a religious purpose. You came to teach us – not to talk about God."

That explained why their first essays had God in every sentence.

Peter said, "I was surprised to see a white lady when I came to class and one that was small. I said to myself, 'She's going to have trouble. She's not big enough to handle us', but you commanded respect. I don't want to sound racial, but I couldn't help but notice you didn't talk about God every minute like all the other white people passing through."

"I was shocked I had a white teacher," said Jahmai. "I thought is this for real? All the white people they would bring to the institution come to talk about God. Nobody actually came to do anything that I thought would be significant to my life at that point in time. I already thought I had a relationship with God. I prayed. I did wrong. I knew I wasn't evil. I didn't have the patience for the lectures and the church services because I felt I could just pray on my own and get something done."

There were other surprises for my students.

"Students formed a bond, and you weren't a boss or a dictator. We could ask questions and express ourselves," said Peter.

"If we would have used the textbook alone, it would have been plain and boring and more like a school and it might not have opened up enough avenues for everyone to get through," said Jahmai. "I liked how you brought articles about the different islands, articles like the one about Christopher "Dudus" Coke in Jamaica.

"By you bringing your own work, you felt out all your students. It's not that everyone liked all the topics, but someone would relate to something and someone would open other students' minds about what it was he liked. Variety and relevance…Not everyone in class would like the same songs you brought to teach us instead of poems all the time. Marc really liked 'Hallelujah'. Some liked Bob Marley or Soca music. The same with reading and literature…The books you chose were because of our interests. You asked us what we liked to read.

"You brought the Tim Tebow book for Olton because he liked rugby and everyone got something they needed and we got to see another side of things. You brought a biography of Jay-Z and that gave Shawn the opportunity to come out of his shell. We noticed how you always brought something for everyone's interests, and I think the variety of the material helped us to feel more comfortable and express ourselves better," said Jahmai.

"Everyone was finding himself instead of a teacher trying to have the same constant all the same time. To me, everything was being taught at once, grammar, reading, writing, but it didn't feel like a burden. It didn't feel overwhelming. You made everyone feel special."

In class, they had learned that everyone had an invaluable contribution to make, and I hoped they would carry that lesson out into the "real" world.

"Kheelon wasn't one of the strongest in the class. When asked to write about himself, he used sports to show how he has confidence, and you read his essay to the class. We realised we performed at different levels, but you made us feel the same and you used work from all of us and showed us how different essays worked – why they were good – so that we all felt we could learn from each other," said Jahmai.

Olton said, "I wanted to do English because I felt it would help me on the outside to get a better job and so I would be proud of myself that I got the pass. It helped me with situations inside of YTC – with officers always quarrelling with me and me always getting in trouble. I had something constructive to do when I started going to class. I looked forward to the class to get out of the dorms. Everybody was learning different things: how to speak, how to use more advanced words.

"The class worked because everyone was comfortable. We laughed and had fun. We talked about things in life. We could argue a point, and we talked to one another. I was shocked. I didn't know I could read so many books: *Uncommon*, *The Blind Side*, Tim Tebow's book *Through My Eyes*," said Olton.

My students not only appreciated each other, but also realised how much they came to rely on one another.

"In class, everybody was important to me," said Olton. "You have to get other people's visions or you can't get all the different sides of information. No one person defined the class or made the class exciting or happy. Everyone was important. Sometimes if one person didn't come, you could see the mood would be different. Different people had the class going. Class was like a family. We spent so much time together."

When I think of a prison, I think of endless time to study. I was never aware of the challenges my students faced when it came to studying.

"Concentrating is hard," said Peter. "There are 20 of us in a dorm. The TV is on all the time. There's constant noise. No one cares if you're studying. Sometimes you find time to study late at night. The light is on day and night so you can study any time. You learn to block out the noise to study just like you learn how to block out the light and the noise to sleep," said Peter.

I wondered how students like Kheelon had survived academically in those conditions and what English class had meant to him considering his exam was a nightmare.

"To tell you the truth, Miss, I never took any English classes at a secondary school level until I came to your class in YTC. I didn't pass the exam. I don't know if I had any chance because I was upset when the guard came in between the two exams and accused me of taking a cell phone, but I got a lot out of class," said Kheelon.

"The most important thing I learned was how to put thoughts into my own words. Taking things from my own experiences helped me. You gave me assignments on sports to do because you realised that was my strong point.

"I had trouble writing and then I realised my thoughts came faster than my hand could write. I learned to slow down my thoughts so I could keep up with writing about them. When I went back inside to the dorms after class, I spent time with myself studying what you taught me. I practiced everything, and if I didn't know something, I asked Shawn."

I had always felt each student had his own individual journey, and he did, but I had not realised how close they had been to each other.

"Jahmai and I became friends under negative activities," said Peter. "We were constantly giving trouble in YTC. For a while, when Jahmai was on remand we were together, and then we were in the cell blocks together when we gave trouble.

"So Jahmai and I were always talking about all the negative things we did out there. Then we got fed up talking about that. How much can you talk about that? We started to talk about family and girls, and then we came around to talking about school. The first thing on your mind in here is freedom, and after awhile you realise freedom is a long way off, and I began to realise I could do something to better myself.

"Jahmai vouched for me when Ms McDonald came around and asked if there was anyone he thought could handle an English class. Jahmai looked at me and said, 'He's a good fellow.' I came to class because of Jahmai, for something to do. I stayed because I found as a teacher, you were down to earth. You listened to us; listened to our problems in life. Class came like it was escape time from the prison itself. It was like we actually got out of the entire prison for a time. Class gave us something different to talk about other than our crimes."

Eventually, Jahmai would be released from YTC and Peter would be left behind in YTC.

"I was glad for Jahmai to go out there because I know a man won't be locked up forever and then if you go out there I could tell if you're really my friend and Jahmai is. He sends messages with his family and you, Miss. 'Stay strong. Stay focused.' He always tries to motivate me."

It's enough to keep Peter going.

Olton's Story

I looked up from my desk in the school library where I work, and saw a smiling Olton framed in the doorway. He had decided to give me a surprise visit on his 20th birthday. Olton had no big plans for the day, just to go on Facebook to see if anyone sent any birthday greetings.

I have never known Olton to be without a smile. Even when he was in YTC, Olton was the boy who always beamed a smile. He's as soft natured as he is large and fit. He's a rugged, rugby player, and he learned about rugby and books in YTC.

"I was a cricketer before I came to YTC. When I came into the cellblocks a boy said, 'You're big enough to play rugby' so I played rugby," said Olton.

He was chosen for the Trinidad and Tobago National Under-20 rugby team, and he got many opportunities to travel everywhere from England to the Cayman Islands and Mexico.

It never seemed that someone like Olton could be in trouble. He took care of his sickly stepmother, running errands for her and doing most of the chores from the time he was 12 until she died. But boys can find trouble.

"One day, a friend saw me in town and asked me if I want jewellery to buy. I paid for it, and police arrested me. They told me they were stolen items, and they locked me up in May 2009. I got three years. I set my mind to do good," says Olton.

Olton came into YTC the same time as Jahmai. They were in the same batch – "…60–69. That's my batch," says Olton. "Jahmai was 63 and I was 65."

"Jahmai's personality was different from mine, but we still got along. We talked a lot and tried to see things and we had one focus: we wanted to go out there and do something better in life. When he was in hard times I would help him out and when I had hard times he helped me. We helped out each other. When we were reading books he'd say, 'Batch come and read this.' We'd show each other different things, metaphors, similes…."

Olton exuded confidence. "I said to myself I'm sure I'm passing that exam. That's how I am. I tell myself 'Pass,' and that's what I do. I say something before I get it. I am a confident person. If I get something wrong, I get it wrong, but that's how life is. I was sure even with all the people there the first class I would be in the class. I was sure because that is what I wanted."

Olton always follows the same philosophy: "Try to be simple. Don't look for petty things. If you keep life simple, you can be humble."

He works now as a security guard, waking up at 4:00 a.m. to get to work for 6 – if he's working the day shift. Each work day is 12 hours long.

"During the day, I stand out in the hot sun and take car numbers as people drive in the compound. I get lonely working nights, but my mind runs through a lot of things: sports, the future, friends. I don't go anywhere. I don't go to parties. I work or stay home. Saving my money is important to me," says Olton.

Olton desperately wants to find a way to play rugby, but fears losing his job.

"I'm afraid to tell them at work I'm a national player. They might fire me or push me in another job with less money. I have to work for money so I might have to give up rugby for a while because I have a next life to live."

Olton didn't do any other subjects in YTC besides CXC English language because he banked on rugby as his salvation. Still, he's satisfied he took all the opportunities he could in YTC.

"I saw how I was outside, nothing really in my life, and I thought I couldn't come inside and not take advantage of all the things they have to offer inside YTC. You don't want to go outside with nothing because outside too hard. You don't want to go back inside there either. It's like you're just wasting time and wasting your life in there. Prison is not a nice place."

"It's a little hard. It hurts I can't play rugby, but in life you make choices. Right now, I have no choice. I have to work."

Another year older, another year wiser: Olton, the softest soul to ever come out of YTC, spent his birthday with me.

Life is a Masquerade

Sometimes I wonder how much we really know about anyone who is in our lives. We think we know how someone thinks or feels, but the more I knew about these boys, the less I often understood them. They were full of surprises at every stage of their academic journey. How much did I really see? What did I really know about the time they had spent with me?

"It's a mas we all were playing," says Jahmai. "Things weren't how they looked. I had decided to come to class because I needed an English and mathematics pass. I believe my thinking pattern had changed, by then, but not my actions. I wanted to do better, but I was still getting in a lot of fights. I still wanted to wear the mask. I hoped class would last. I didn't want to think about coming out of YTC and doing CXC outside with much younger students. I wanted to be doing what people my age would be doing even though I was inside prison so I needed English language class to work for me.

"I needed you to stay. I needed students in the class with certain standards so you would stay. I didn't want anyone in the class to act out. I wanted to say, 'This one is serious. She wants to teach us.' I wanted certain people not to be there because I knew that would be like a flaw in my plan. I was trying to feel out everyone.

"In class, we could talk about what we were studying. I liked the work in class, but as I left the classroom, I had to put on a different face. Survival. That's what it all came down to the instant you got back to the dorm. You're thinking how to get your hands on a phone; if you can get a cigarette;

how you can get something good to eat. You're bartering right through like something in *Shawshank Redemption*.

"When we would go to class, we started watching life from a different perspective; that you have to do certain things in life because it's the right thing to do.

"I surprised myself that I stayed so long in class. I knew I had the potential because I had reached Form Four before I came into YTC. I just never settled down to do what I had to do out there in class. My focus was on making dollars.

"Even in lockdown, I submitted work because it was part of the plan. I was not to be in lockdown. I needed to be in that class. I had to do more. When they sent me to lockdown I was like *this can't reflect good on me*. It's hindering my plan, and I didn't want you to judge me by what was said about me by the authorities. I wanted my voice to be heard. I wanted to make my own impression. I thought this looks bad. Here I got into the class, and now I'm in lockdown. I needed to get back in class. I used to actually beg Mr Stewart – mamaguy him in a sense – going to any extreme to go to get back in the class. Mr Stewart was like, 'You give me trouble in the institution and you can't get what you want.' Guards said they were getting bad reports of the company I was keeping and the things I was doing.

"I knew I was at a disadvantage being out of the class. I remember Friday used to come outside of lockdown and shout down the corridor what we did in class, saying even the jokes students shared. I always wanted to not know what was going on. I wanted to feel everything in class.

"I tried to do a lot of reading like you said. The reading I did helped me to be creative. I enjoyed the thinking patterns of fictional characters. It was my way of meeting new people. I could see them in my mind and my imagination. When I read *Jane Eyre*, I actually met her and felt what she felt. I remember how humble she was. Reading allowed me to meet different types of people and understand how they think and feel.

"Reading gave me opportunities to meet people who were not Trinidadians. That helped with my writing. Reading expanded my mind, and helped my ability to accept things, and it even helped my writing speed. My biggest worry was I couldn't write fast enough and the more I read and the better I got at reading, I realised it really did help with writing speed.

"Reading also gave me the opportunity to go places even when I was in lockdown. No one could take away my independence. In *King Solomon's Mines* – I got to go to Africa. I liked classics. I liked how the characters spoke. Their tone wasn't modern. It came like it was before all the mess in my life. What was modern represented what I was in. Classics were a way to express some kind of comfort in the past.

"What surprised me by the end of the class was how everyone in class started looking out for each other when you made the final cut. I never thought we'd come together like that or that we would help each other to express ourselves. The class worked because I was determined it had to work. It worked because of the changes I started to see in the characters in the class, helping each other like opening up a different side like they wouldn't open up in the dormitories.

"You knew what we would feed off of and take and run with. We came to learn and feed off of each other. I was of the impression that we connected so much that you thought if I bring this to class they'll feed off this. There are so many different books you could have brought, but why did you bring a particular book on this day? Why did you bring the first book first and not make that the last? It was like we were building something together.

"Class did change us. We never tried to use too much slang after your classes. When we spoke to each other, we tried to practise speaking. I viewed the class as something new. I like new adventures. It started coming across I wasn't alone in trying to make this work.

"After we left the classroom it was going back to a reality that you had to do for yourself. It wasn't like you're going back home and everything is there waiting for you. After that hour (7 p.m.) even food was an issue so we put on our masks again.

"In the dorms, the other guys just saw going to class as us finding a way to get out of the dorm. That, they understood. Those who were more victims in the dorm rather than role models would get made fun of for going to class. They wouldn't make fun of me, Marc, Shawn or Peter.

"They would pong Olton about his education, about going to classes because of his personality. I believe he never wore the mask after class. He was Olton the same in classroom and outside, that naïveté and optimism he always had. At some point in time they'd give a jab because they knew he could take it and laugh it off. To me, that helped fuel me a lot. That helped me to keep quiet. It was a lesson in itself observing how Olton would move. Even if someone would say the worst to him, he would never react. He would never respond. He would accept wrong for what other people did. He never had the voice or the grounding to say he didn't know or couldn't do something. He would be cheery even in the face of trouble.

"For Olton, English class was deeper than academic accomplishment. He wanted to have the information to share. He'd always say he had to know this for his child some day. At his game, he was one of the best. He was always recognised because of his rugby. No one tried to hold down his accomplishments because he was so positive. He never tried to keep down anyone. He was too down to earth. He would have his moments where he would be sad or angry but his angry moments would be the start of his sad moments. His angry moments would identify all he didn't have. If there was anyone I could not have a second thought about, it would probably be him.

"That was Olton. For the rest of us, we'd put on the mask when we went back to the dorm so that we could feel accepted again. We would mention that English class does something for us. We would say that we have a plan to try education as a means of going forward, and we'd talk about it in a way that it wouldn't feel like something hard. We'd say, 'Hey we're going to class,' but it was in a certain tone, like we're going to bathe.

"They'd say, 'What that class have in it boy?' There was envy – not of the class – but envy of the person. We used to strut around the place with an extra level of confidence. We always said we have a plan, but we wouldn't say we're going to get out of there with passes.

"I actually didn't tell anyone I got my CXC passes. I didn't want anyone to feel like it's nothing that I got. I knew it meant something, and not everyone can be a well-wisher. People tend to try to compete. I didn't want to feel like I was in that competition with the rest. It's like society: Everyone competing. It's not like they put us in a place not in Trinidad or not on this earth."

All Alone

In the end, there was only Peter left for me to teach English. He had decided to sit the CXC English literature exam along with Ralph. Ralph sat the exam in June 2012. Peter would sit the exam in June 2013.

Alone and working in a vacuum, a class of one, with no one at his academic level other than Ralph, Peter persevered. Although he produced excellent work, Peter doubted his ability to do English literature. His confidence in general sometimes waned and, understandably, he sometimes became despondent, but Peter always found a way to rally. On days when I feel life is daunting; on days when I feel we all take life a little too much for granted, I think of Peter, alone with his dreams and aspirations. Peter wants to be a lawyer one day.

One day, I shared Peter's story with the staff at my school, and they wrote these letters:

Hello Peter,

I have heard so much about you from Ms Jacob that in a way I feel like I know you. She has shared with me the admiration and respect that she has for you on a number of levels. I was struck not only by the academic ability that she describes, but also by how passionate she is about what you have taught her about life. I was a little surprised at first as she's the teacher, but she seems to have learnt so much from her interactions with you over the last couple years.

I too am an English teacher, so I paid attention when Ms Jacob told me how well you are doing and that she thinks you are capable of getting a 1 on your CXC literature exam. She also shared with me how articulate you are and how well you write.

I couldn't help thinking of one of my treasured pieces The Autobiography of Malcolm X. *I remember when I was first reading it many, many years ago I first felt sympathy for young Malcolm Little as he really was a victim of discrimination and violence with his father being killed and his mother being forced into a mental home. He had to live in a detention home for a while after that, before going to live with a relative.*

He had only attained up to a form 2 or 3 level of education and wasn't exactly literate, however as he developed I didn't like Malcolm Little the young man much at all. He became a young man into his clothes, gambling, women, drugs and also armed robbery. He eventually landed in prison. That, however, turned out to be what saved him.

I don't know if you know his story, but the reason that I love this book so much is because of the lesson it holds about the power of education to transform and the power of love to do the same. Malcolm became educated in prison: he hungered for knowledge and I remember finding it amusing that one of the first things he did was to "learn" the dictionary; he studied English, read voraciously and even joined the prison debate team. Malcolm X has taken his place in history and inspired so many along the way. He made a difference. We truly never know when our lives will be used as an inspiration to others.

Please continue working and persevering and learning. One day you may be called upon and you need to be ready. What better person to be a lawyer than someone who has experienced both sides of the law?

I have pasted one of my favourite poems below.

All the best in your exams in May and beyond.

Charmaine Quamina

"Dreams"
by Langston Hughes

Hold fast to dreams
For if dreams die
Life is a broken-winged bird
That cannot fly.
Hold fast to dreams
For when dreams go
Life is a barren field
Frozen with snow.

Dear Peter,

I'm sitting here on a Tuesday morning in my classroom feeling the need for a little inspiration. Ideas for new ways to approach old subjects are hard to find and finding the drive to really look hard for those ideas can be harder still.

So I take a break and I read an email from someone we both know very well. She tells me about a young man who has faced more adversity than I can comprehend and yet still fights every day to better himself. What does this do to me? It wakes me up. It tells me that I need to do more, that I need to show just a measure of the character that you are showing to your teacher at YTC.

To say that I am impressed by your ambition and your drive isn't enough, it makes me want to work harder, to push myself, because while I am doing a good job, I could do a hell of a lot more. I hope you stay the course and stick with your studies. If you can keep pushing forwards then you'll inspire so many others to do the same, all your hard work gives you the opportunity to show the world what you are really made of, so keep pushing on as it'll open doors and break down walls for you.

All the Best
Mathew Broughtton

Dear Peter,

I am the basketball coach at the Beetham (one of the poorest areas in Trinidad) where I live, and I run the weekend basketball programme, The Warriors. I am also a PE teacher at the International School of Port of Spain.

On many occasions I have visited Carrera (the prison for long-term inmates located on a small island off Trinidad's shores). Whenever I go to Carrera, I see guys who just disappeared from the Beetham and I would think oh, this is what happened to them. One of my basketball players was involved in the Tackle Shop murder years ago. He didn't shoot, but he was in the car. He is in his 30s now and doing life.

When I talked to those guys in Carrera, I realised they're really not so bad. They just got caught up in things – caught up in another life outside and having to play the game inside. They're fighting for survival first outside of and then inside of jail. Life should be about more than just surviving so here is my advice to you:

Know it is very important to get your education. If you come out with passes, it will help you to get a better job. Life is real hard without an education. It limits your options.

Remember who you really are. I know how you have to act sometimes like everyone else, play the game inside there to survive, but don't lose track of who you really are.

You have a lot of time on your hands to read and study. Don't lose sight of that.

We go through many stages in our lives, but you can't give up. Sometimes it looks like there's no way out, but by not giving up you are moving forward.

Keep positive. Keep your head on your shoulders. Inside of there can make you feel negative. Pray a lot. That gives you strength.

Find something good in your life, something that makes you laugh. Think of those things sometimes when you feel down. Just keep positive. Negativity inside there could send you crazy.

You have to live with a sense of hope. If you don't live with hope you don't live with anything. Anything can happen with hope.

Sincerely,
Albert Sprott

Dear Peter,

I have heard so many good things about you and your achievements, about your life and about how you are a wonderful young man. You see my mother, Ms Jacob, is your teacher and she has painted a colourful and exciting picture of you, a young man who has had to overcome so many obstacles in his life, obstacles I could never begin to understand.

I have been given the opportunity to hear about your ability to succeed and rise despite the circumstances you have endured. You may not know this, but my mother speaks of you as a mother would her child. She feels for you when you get discouraged and celebrates with you when you succeed. My mother's renditions of her time spent with you have enabled me to think of you as a brother, one that has had a different life and different circumstances, but shares the same mother as I do.

As your sister, I feel you deserve to know that I get inspiration and strength from you. Your perseverance and strength has allowed me to see the hope on the horizon, and I am confident that the strength that lies within you and the knowledge that one day you will be set free to achieve wonderful things in this world will prevail. Keep the faith and stay strong. Find your freedom in the books you read. Remember that when you are stripped of your worldly belongings and titles you are no longer forced to be owned by them and must now own yourself and create your own destiny.

"Confront the dark parts of yourself, and work to banish them with illumination and forgiveness. Your willingness to wrestle with your demons will cause your angels to sing. Use the pain as fuel, as a reminder of your strength"– August Wilson

Sincerely,
Ijanaya

The Last Say

Everything changes. Life goes on. I do not know what happened to all of the 27 students who first came to class. I know at least three of them are back in prison. Dorian is dead. JR is working as an electrician and hoping to follow his passion: cooking. Some of the students are still in YTC serving their sentences. At the time I write this CP, one of the original 27 students has five more months of his sentence.

I still regret giving up CP as a student. He wanted to be a doctor. One of my most eager students, CP needed serious remedial work, and to keep him would have been unfair to everyone.

While in YTC, CP got his certification to be an electrician, and someone is trying to set him up with a job as soon as he comes out of YTC.

"I hope to be able to rent a place when I get out," CP told me, "because I have nowhere to go."

"No sisters or brothers?" I asked.

"They're very poor, Miss," he said. "My sister has a baby and she lives in a shack."

I thought about the day CP had come to tell me that his mother had been murdered. "Were you close to your mother?" I asked him one dark night as I was waiting for a guard to let me out of the school.

"I had written her a letter just before she was murdered. I never got the chance to give it to her," said CP.

"She knows how you felt," I said.

CP laughed, and I realised how trite I sounded.

No one has been arrested for the murder of CP's mother.

There isn't a week that goes by when I don't hear about a boy who has gone to a funeral: a mother who is killed; a sister who is raped and killed – someone is always killed.

Here is the final word, as of August 18, 2013 on my other students:

Ashton's case was finally heard and reduced to manslaughter. He received a sentence of 16 years, and credit for time served in YTC. He is pursuing his education and teaching Social Studies in Maximum Security Prison. I am able to visit Ashton from time to time. He will be out of prison in 2014.

Miguel's case had been heard and reduced to manslaughter before he attended CXC English class. As I write this in 2013, he continues to serve the additional five-year sentence the court gave him. He will be out of prison in 2014.

Peter, 20, is still waiting for his case to be heard. In August 2013, Peter received a "One" in English Literature. He now has four CXC passes. We are currently doing CXC Caribbean History, and then we plan to tackle CAPE subjects.

Ralph, 24, is still waiting for his case to be heard. In March 2013, he finally went to court and found out the police officer in charge of his case was no longer working. Another police officer had to be assigned the case. In court, he learned that his two lawyers had quit, and he would have another court-appointed lawyer. Ralph has been waiting seven years for his trial.

Since his release, Shawn has been attending university-level classes. In the middle of the night, we often connect on Facebook while Shawn works on a project. On Carnival Tuesday 2013, Shawn, a relative and three friends stayed home "to make a cook" so that they could avoid trouble. While pursuing a suspect running through the area, police stormed Shawn's house without a search warrant and arrested everyone after they lost the suspect they were chasing. Police charged all five young men with possession of marijuana, possession of a weapon (gun) and possession of ammunition. Shawn says he is innocent.

Kheelon is working and playing football.

Vaughn is working and trying to further his studies.

Marc is working off and on and still hopes to be a writer.

In August 2013, Jahmai was accepted to the University of the West Indies. He wants to be a social worker.

Olton works and still wants to find a way to play rugby.

There is rarely a day that goes by without Marc, Olton, Shawn, Jahmai or Kheelon contacting me. Every morning I read their messages on Facebook.

They write, "Have a nice day, Miss" or "I am thinking of you."

Sometimes they write, "Thank you for everything you did for me," or "I'll never forget you, Miss."

Often, they write, "I love you, Miss."

I reply, "Right back at you."

Then I go out into the world with a feeling of hope.

Acknowledgements

I once felt like Daedalus piecing together wings out of birds' feathers and wax so that he and his son, Icarus could escape from the prison King Minos had built after Daedalus completed the Labyrinth to house the Minotaur.

I was fortunate enough to have the support of kind and knowledgeable people to prevent me from making Daedalus's mistake. These are the people who provided the glue for me to hold everything together so that my students at YTC would not follow in the path of Icarus, who flew too close to the sun and melted his wings.

To me, these caring individuals feel like characters in an ancient Greek myth.

Mathematics teacher Gwendolyn Pope knew I could handle the formula for flying long before I did. Arthur Dash, my former editor at the *Trinidad Guardian*, gently nudged me to the edge of my comfort zone by encouraging me to write columns in the *Trinidad Guardian* about the lost boys of Trinidad. Anthony Wilson, acting Editor in Chief of the *Trinidad Guardian* when I began writing my columns, propelled me to move forward with his editorial support. Judy Raymond, the current Editor in Chief of the *Guardian* has been an unwavering source of encouragement throughout the entire process of making wings. She kept me connected to my journalistic roots. The *Trinidad Guardian* generously provided paper for wings and a launching pad for our trial runs.

Friend, writer, journalist and Attorney-at-Law, Kathy Ann Waterman, challenged me to spread my wings and write more than the *Guardian* series. My son, Jairzinho never began his Saturday night lime until I came home from YTC. I am grateful for his smile, the first I saw every weekend after my many test flights at YTC.

My daughter, Ijanaya, understood the loneliness I felt when she flew away to university to become a fashion designer. Her unwavering support helped me to leave our family's nest every weekend and fashion wings with pride.

Unlike Daedalus, I was never alone with my secret plans to make wings. Students of the International School of Port of Spain organised bake sales and teachers bought books my students needed to prepare for flight.

Louis Moore, Alicia Solozano, John Horsfall, Marie Chan Durity, Karena Amow, Suzette Julien, Yves and Allison Johnson, Amelia Parkes, Albert Sprott, Nadira Akal, Maeve O'Donovan, Matthew Broughtton, Anthony Blackburn, Rebecca Tompsett, Momeda Khan, and many other members of staff at the International School of Port of Spain offered emotional, academic and financial support – never-ending glue sticks that helped me hold everything together.

My assistant, Nicha Cassiram, kept my flighty self organised for class, and she e-mailed me every Saturday night anxious to hear about my latest ventures.

Former Minister of Education, Mrs Hazel Manning, read my columns and wrote the most appreciative and inspiring letter that I received in this endeavour. I will always keep that letter tucked under my wing.

Mr Sterling Stewart, the Supervisor of YTC and Donna McDonald gave me total freedom to experiment with my flying lessons. They possessed none of King Midas's fears. Trinidad and Tobago prisons' social worker Roderick Beaumont helped me navigate my way through the social issues generally associated with young men who end up in prison. When it comes to support, he is as solid as a rock.

Wendell Manwarren of 3canal provided my students and me with maps of their unfamiliar surroundings when he bought my students copies of *Miguel Street* by V.S. Naipaul.

All the young men in my CXC English language class and Ralph in CXC English literature class knew of and lived the story of Daedalus and Icarus yet they were bold enough to fly as close to the sun as they could, never doubting my vision.

Birds on their first flight need a cheering section. Countless *Guardian* readers commented on the columns and registered their support. We heard the echo of those voices on our test flights. Althea Phillip from Royal Bank gathered funds for books to launch my students on their latest dreams.

Publishing a book feels like a mother bird releasing her nestlings. Every mother bird stands by anxiously and helplessly hoping that her birds will not merely tumble from the sky. The fear and agony of waiting for a response from a publisher is indescribable.

I was lucky to choose the best place in the world for us all to land: Ian Randle Publishers. Ian Randle immediately responded to my query and my manuscript, telling me that he had read the manuscript on a train from Amsterdam to Paris while Christine Randle gave a quick and enthusiastic thumbs up in Kingston.

Books inspire me, and although I have never met these authors, I owe them a great deal for providing the courage anyone needs to fly: Tony Dungy taught my students and me what it meant to be *Uncommon*. Leigh Anne and Sean Tuohy were there *In a Heart Beat* showing us the art of cheerful giving, and Michael Oher provided us with a survival guide in *I Beat the Odds: From Homelessness to the Blind Side* and Beyond. I am ever mindful that Guyanese writer Edward Ricardo Brathwaite laid the groundwork for my work at YTC in his timeless novel *To Sir with Love*.

I could fill an entire book thanking everyone who helped

and supported me in this venture. That includes everyone who reads this book because all of my royalties will go towards helping these young men land on their feet as they make their way back into Trinidad society.

No one's support will ever be taken for granted.

Thanks to all for the crazy glue. Because of you, Icarus flies.

CPSIA information can be obtained at www.ICGtesting.com
Printed in the USA
BVOW08s2013250216

437893BV00002B/11/P